Complete Poetic Works

Kokyo David Young

for my wife, Ruby

&

for Shannon & James Fraser

Kokyo David Edgar Young was the final child of Dr. & Mrs. John Alexander FRASER Young of Pictou Nova Scotia . After the tragic death of his father in a car accident in 1969 and the subsequent death of his mother Kathleen (Cassie) ne: Pope; in 1972; on March 24th, 1973 David married Ruby Judith Young, daughter of Mr. & Mrs. Sam (Lucy) Wong.

Ruby and David have a son, Shawn, who became a carpenter and married Karen Gerrior, giving David & Ruby a wonderful granddaughter, Emily Judith Young in 2005.

In 2007, David, following up on a life-long interest in Buddhism, formally became a Zen Buddhist, joining the Sangha of the Atlantic Soto Zen Center, Halifax, as a lay practitioner.

David struggled with bipolar disorder, which he overcame with "meditation & medication".
David and Ruby currently live in Pictou.

He wishes to thank his dear Nephew, Darryl Wong, without whom this compilation could not have been accomplished. Also to be thanked are Ruby, for her devotion, and all those who supported and encouraged him in his work.

Nature Discovers Itself

It was as if

An eloquent flower

Had become conscious,

And went raving about its own beauty.

It was as though the brook

Suddenly babbled words

Moreover, mountains thundered

Their announcement of the day

Grown aware of itself;

Through the empty poet,

Bereft of man's grasping,

Hailing the newly awakened day!

~ Kokyo

After Clarence

Sighting the white berries

That could have poisoned baby Grace

I think of our tumultuous summer.

With Clarence gone and you returned home,

Aunt Judy and I remember in winter's silence...

~ Kokyo

After the Rain

After the rain

I walk through the streets,

in the freshness.

The rain soaked leaves

Wash away pain;

A cloud burst assuages it.

In the freshness I walk,

Unencumbered by device.

There is not cunning in my greeting;

Except as much as would lead you consider,

The freshness left by the rain...

~ Kokyo

Annie at the Flicks

Annabel Limpton,

haggled and freshly vomited,

has left her room of sun-stained curtain lace,

to foggle-eye the celluloid depiction

of the blinking perception

of John Dustin, director-producer.

Will John touch little Annie,

her eye-lashes falling

as she stutters home

at flick's end?

~ Kokyo

Chalice

It's late, and you've gone,

but I must stay where you've been;

Thinking of cellophane ballerinas,

Arlo Gruthrie and talk of Montreal.

Tomorrow I must be a pallbearer,

For your eyes were a chalice when I held them

And saw my image there; and that was union,

Till my falling eyes dropped the cup,

The ballerina crumbled —a fool's dream

Dispersed among the scattered shells

of a broken goblet.

~ Kokyo

For My Brother Jon

Amusing myself with thoughts,

Or lapsing into joyous serenity –

It doesn't matter

Dipping water into moonlight water:

Lap...lap...lap...

~ Kokyo

For Ruby

Intending to soothe it with tenderness,

Rather I have ravished your heart with sorrow.

Attempts to understand elude me;

Abandoning them, I leave the domain of earth –

Finding that I have loved you all along

In that pure, sweet way, I wished.

I am sorry for the sadness.

But, beyond earth, I will heal your sorrow now,

Leading you, from within, into gladness.

~ Kokyo

Goose/Bottle

Birds sing –

poems ensue!

~ Kokyo

Haiku on Pearl's Death

The blistered hand

that did your gardening

is healed...

Now there is no trace of you.

~ Kokyo

Love

Love audaciously

Ride the exquisite horse of love with valor,

Give her rein; use the stirrup, never the whip.

Risk the hurdles; finish the course

Gather the garland

Putting love foremost, sacrifice all;

Should you fall, never regret mounting,

Never decline the chase!

~ Kokyo

Huang Po

We speak, yet each word defiles it,

Yet we speak.

Obaku spoke it all

His mouth never uttering a word

Mind revolves through mind

The two being one

When mind exhausts itself

Mind appears

In the very workings of mind

Creating a great humanism

Laughter and hope

Joy lies at the bottom of every movement.

Mind continues to work its plan

Even in the midst of apparent

Great suffering

**Huang
Po**

Its creation is vast, immense -

It goes to the very marrow, yet

Flutters as a leaf on top of still waters.

It is through mind that one approaches Mind,

moving dyanamically throughout your being:

Even in the most momentous hurricane,

Not one leaf falls to the ground...

~ Kokyo

I do not know

the one

who is saying

now

that he does not know

the one

who has said

he does not know

the one

who says he does not know...

~ Kokyo

Affinities

I share an affinity,

With the broken...

Stones rejected by the builders.

With which we build our inner temples,

Sheltering the entire world...

~ Kokyo

Joshu

Intent in heart,

In early morning,

I look toward the awakening world,

Filled with a joyous, tender compassion.

The sun rises; the sky clears.

As friends come calling, I serve breakfast –

Have a cup of tea!

~ Kokyo

I've found my Home

Lilacs bloom outside our window

In our comfortable old home,

I have built myself a study.

Whiling away the hours reading D. T. Suzuki,

Rain drops clinging to leaves,

After this morning's shower.

~ Kokyo

Jade Fish

(For Robert and Wade)

Wearing a Jade Fish, given to me by my wife,

That morning, I went up to New Hope.

There I met a man from New Beginnings,

Who was blind, but who had vision,

No eyes can see!

He felt the fish and we thus

Identified ourselves to each other

In the manner of the early Christian Mystics.

Refreshed,

I left there thinking about,

That inner garden of Joy,

we need no eyes to see...

~ Kokyo

Loss, a homeward going spirit

The heart departs,

 Oscillating to a refreshed composure.

Beyond travail – joy unbounded.

The singer retires; the song ends...

The universe has pollinated –

I flower!

The rest is mercy...

~ Kokyo

Moon

White mercury of mid-winter,

Deal me the face of the void -

As I sing out,

The uncreated emanations of my nature!

~ Kokyo

My Ruby

You have strewn petals on my way, softening my steps with love.

Gasping as I fell; holding your breath

As I regained my footing.

Flimsy words cannot hold the ocean of devotion

I carry in my deep heart;

Allow me to pour it, please, soothingly,

Into yours...

~ Kokyo

Nestle

Lay your troubled head upon my chest

I will not give you sorrow any more.

It is quickly approaching mid-night

Do not dream your dreams without my

Presence

You will not lift your eyes

To find my hand not with yours.

I will gladly line the channels

Of your next approach with my love...

I will eradicate the pain, which was pain I have given you!

~ Kokyo

Nothing could bring me

To empty myself of you

For, days emptying into one another,

My heart resonates an assurance –

A tale more beautiful

In living than in telling...

~ Kokyo

On Compassion for My Wife

If you scoop up

A handful of flower petals,

Getting as many as you can;

It is inevitable,

That some will fall!

~ Kokyo

Polish

There are those who,

living 400 miles away,

dwell here in my heart.

Old friends pass my home,

pursuing their careers;

They have their satisfactions –

I have poetry,

and the hardships of true living...

Joys gather around my heart,

as the one who has climbed these years with me –

steadfast, devoted, weakened –

proffers her cheek in her alluring manner;

then polishes our sparse silver,

as she has polished our marriage

all these long, rich, full years...

~ Kokyo

Ruby and I

The world is new this morning –

The dew hung on my heart,

And you, resonating through the void!

Dave

Scalpel

Hate you?

Well, not actively, except for this;

And hatred, rather like fungus

on a stout healthy sausage,

or a bloated tumor, or a mind's dusty floor,

must be scraped away –

Hence this scalpel.

And you, sausage-eater-

You hurl your hatred onward towards its object;

Its object because it objected to being your predicate –

I not being an attribute of you.

I must affirm what you deny –

My existence apart from yours

O great man-eater!

~ Kokyo

Seeing the Moon

Pain...hour by hour...agony...

Hope kindles...compassion surges...

Climbing the stairs to the night air –

The moments mounting to eternity...

The culmination of all my ages,

The birth of a new being

When, at that slight off-glance –
I saw the moon...

Descending, awareness broke,
Beauty splashing over the heart,
Redounding over the entire world...

~ Kokyo

Something Informs the Tall Green Grass

We have only inklings of the magnificence
Of what we are doing;
My eyes have reddened on unalterable day.

The orb of my philosophy is threatened by fire.
Let the cold weather break before we damage
The face we put on the void.

Something informs the tall green grass,

Alive its sway.

Adsorbed in the milky tones of your voice;

My eyes sewn with the sinews of your display.

Among the stars our tales resound,

As we open out like flowers to the sun.

It has been assured: thought the road is long,

The old lady is ever at the teahouse!

Something...

He has journeyed the heartland;

He has forsaken the coast –

Managing to make of scarcity, a meal.

Your flesh numbed by an experience

Too fearsome to warrant our approach.

Stunned into your persuasion of sustained revelation

Astonished into glee!

Birds fly off at my approach,

As the sawyer builds my gazebo.

Into the forest, tonight, I will trample –

Watching, from the darkness,

The approaching day...

~ Kokyo

Song Bird

I gathered a songbird,

Whose song had ceased,

Her wing having been broken

Into my hand;

It took so long for me to heal her

As my hands trembled

At such a fearsomely delicate task;

But as she has mended,

So my hands have been made steady.

Now, will she fly away

Or stay here with me...

~ Kokyo

Sound Love

Tears fell,

As I watched you boarding,

Your rotting dory, up stream,

On the river of Despair.

Hurriedly, I ran ahead,

Downstream,

Cutting my skin on glass and brambles.

Now I sit, assuredly, at the mouth,

Waiting to cast the net of my Love,

Snatching you from the ocean of Oblivion

Knowing that Love, true and full,

Does not fail to rescue us from,

Despair.

~ Kokyo

Spring Birds in Winter

Should you suffer-

Song birds flutter

Onto your heart's

Craggy branches

~ Kokyo

Suffering/Joy

Sun seared, wind wasted,

Having assayed the depths of suffering-

Everything is always alright!

Suffering is efficacious –

Leading to fulfillment:

Without travel, there is no destination:

No walking, no arriving...

Dark night

Suddenly – moon no longer obscured:

Liberating beauty abounding!

Trees sing with the breeze

The broken-hearted lift their eyes,

Seeking relief;

As compassion seeps up, softly,

Through the evening air-

So we sing, causing no harm.

~ Kokyo

Sunrise Poem

You give to me

I shall give it back to you:

I will give you pebbles,

Sifting the moon through my fingers.

Mounting the steps,

I say 'good-bye' for you;

Drinking water at noon

And loving your daughter at night.

Finding my center

Walking out in the Rain –

The flower eats the sunlight

~ Kokyo

Sunrise

Rays, emanating

From the source of the earth

This verdant earth all around

Cultivated by its foundlings.

So do we as sensitive plants

Bathe in the radiation from our centers

Our leafy-green minds,

Are fed by this sun.

We are the cultivating foundlings,

Of the bidden psychic sunrise –

We do capitulate,

As it breaks the sky.

~ Kokyo

Sunset Poem for Ruby

Perhaps this uncommon sunset tonight

Is a sign of our covenant;

And, as we walk back from

The field where we have been watching,

If I, holding your hand, fall silent;

You know it is because, I have not left the sunset behind;

But hold it, burning warmly, in my hand!

~ Kokyo

The Heart

The fire inside

Is warm-

Controlled in the hearth.

The storm outside continues...

Remaining contained:

In your yearning

Is your peace...

~ Kokyo

The Hut in The Woods

The hut in the woods

Is secure-

It's overgrown underbrush

A mug of coffee

Then a fire

Fire enters my head

At this moment

Consuming my reasons for coming

(Anna is there in the wood-box)

Something beckons from behind

An old story

A lost cabin door in the foggy wood

The Hut in The Woods

(Heaven and earth bending like lovers

To seed a new conception.

Hear them moan!)

The thunder tolls

And I know this as the

Witching phase of my life

Overturning stones

Clearing the brush-

Tomorrow-

The intellect yawns out

For the heart, its lover.

The heart, unsought for'

Or cared for with skill;

Longs to heave an insight into

Its lover, the mind.

The Hut in The Woods

(So much unreality-

Persona after persona

Falling)

Now to this cabin

To wipe off the smile

And put on a grin.

(Totems of mind-stuff

Carved luxuriantly

In over-grown years)

Years too smoothly spun

By Anna –

O, this tiresome, gnawing, bitter pain!

The Hut in The Woods

Alone I come to the cabin,

(My psychic underbrush)

Alone, standing before a searing light,

Hovering like a guillotine,

Taunting like a wicket dog:

Naked before the lord of the coming day.

(This mind-stuff- my baggage-

Already you have hurled it into the fire.

Bits of twinkling glass

Haphazardly arranged in the corner

Already deemed valueless- even by me)

Light of my awakening,

Withhold yourself no longer.

The Hut in The Woods

Hurl headlong

Into the breakup of my day

Giving me matter of green ferns,

Fertile soil;

No longer, let me spin ratiocination,

But, having reflection, let me

Reflect my original home.

Let me, bemused by inner nature,

Subdue hankering distraction.

Let your slashing insight

Crash upon me, leaving me

Whistling back at chirruping birds.

Then leave me sparse.

Leave me only ragged earthy peace,

As found on spring's brown fields.

(A silent lifting of a rock

In a missing corner of a life)

The Hut in The Woods

Anna you no longer exist;

And here am I, mown down,

In a gutter, heart ripped out –

Scanning the sky for peace.

There has not been much

Accumulated by me, but,

Reflecting your sun, I shone!

Now the sun is blackened

And I am turned out of the habitable world...

I participate in naught

But the workings my own mind –

Jagged trees soaked in rain,

The earth buried in thunderous clouds.

The Hut in The Woods

All night long, I agonize

Sleep not forthcoming

(Anxious crawling gnats

Eat at my sleep, leaving me wide eyed –

Surveying my cage.

Empty this infested mind;

Can I put on splendor?

I long for my heart to grow slender,

Like a fine reed!)

Dimly in the haze,

A heart arouses and begins the dance

Of liberation.

Drunken with lack of sleep,

My brain ticks over the contours of my cage.

Was the error this love affair?

Convolutions of past actions

Tumble over like barrels;

The thunder echoing nature's mutuality.

(This night is my mind!

Twigs tapping at the window –

The master enchanter knocking

Through the bulwark of my resistance.)

But, now, as the wind wanes,

Stillness subdues me,

An assurance heaves in its sleep

The Hut in The Woods

I am face to face with thunderous self

Throwing trepidation;

Which I turn back upon a laugh.

Slightly I see the vacuity of its existence,

So long threatening, now whimpering away,

Like poor accosted demi-god.

(I see a field, green in morning dew –

I am struck out of my peevishness,

Into a grand compassion,

A weeping sadness, for a world,

Not overgrown with the grandeur

Of this all sustaining, permeating love...

I struggle to be real, natural man.

Rain streaming refreshes

A now windless night

(Nurturing the creating of something new)

The Hut in The Woods

Rumbling in the distance

Announces the coming being;

Echoes the departure of the slinking hound,

Cast away into oblivion

An assuaging shower sooths

The harmful thick of night;

Sighs of morning,

Earth washed in sorrow,

Awakening in gladness.

Now, in sleep, this absence...

Rising, I am empty headed

Vacant as I perform the promised chore –

Clearing rocks – no disturbance

Not even Anna is here.

The Hut in The Woods

I do not notice

The absence of even the slightest

Habitual pain...

Suddenly, flying rock strikes

Boulder – Clink!

I awake to the unseen world...

A new and wondrous element

This very earth perceived as enchanted land.

A new area, mode of being

The earth opening its arms

The hidden world of wonders

Undeniably the

The true state of enthralling existence

The Hut in The Woods

I sit, gape, laugh, grin

The sun in the valley

All its treasure poured out

Anointing my ragged soul

Into a grateful, resigned mirth.

Closing Poem:

HYMN TO THE UNGARNISHED EARTH

You have ever coaxed me into day

You tirelessly bidding earth.

I have undressed my being

And been girded with

Your fine, green stems;

Your majestic, brown mountains.

The Hut in The Woods

You have bestowed me with rain for tears

Dew to sweeten the elixir

Of the unseen tale you are spinning

(In which I now participate

With glad surrender)

Quickening the flowery display –

This ruddy earth.

Dead, the resistance to your bidding

Gleefully I submit to your prompting

Celebrating all that comes from the void;

Exalting every aspect of this new welcome delight

Unspeakable unfathomable knowledge

The Hut in The Woods

An old man

Returning home at dusk;

Smiling at the setting sun –

His conspirator!

~ Kokyo

The Peak

He left the peak, disheartened.

He'd come often in his youth,

When the sun would beam leafy green

Through the ferns; would hang in the sky

Like a yolk.

Off the rotting pole ravens would fly,

Climbing, vanishing into the clouds,

Fetching tomorrow.

He left the peak, satisfied.

He'd come frequently, turning over his daylight

When rain would soak on verdant ferns;

Clouds like whites would sag in the sky.

To the rotting pole, ravens returned, circling,

Dropping from the clouds,

Retching yesterday.

As he left, the sand beneath,

Was settled firmly upon the beach.   ~Kokyo

The World Writes Itself

This pen is moving.

It is writing something.

What is writing?

And who in the world

Comes to appear so solidly, on paper?

~Kokyo

Tincture

Love, like Kwan Yin,

Allowing the world's tears

Soak unto your sleeve,

Like mist on the lake evaporates,

Blushing the void

A resin remains

Forever fading,

        Into the evening haze...

~Kokyo

Unmindful

Lost amid my own musings,

All attempts to extricate myself unavailing...

Resigned, I roam contentedly through Vastness

Containing Joy and Sorrow.

At one with these, finally;

Happy as blossoms

Blown haphazardly about.

Until falling, at last –

I find my rest among the restlive fallen leaves!

~Kokyo

Walking in my Yard

(For Hil, since she likes it so well)

Like old men, the trees stand –

firm yet unobtrusive.

Perhaps you are sages assembled in my presence.

At any rate, strolling among you at dusk I feel my self,

being empty, is met with no resistance;

my wandering through nature is unhindered

since I pose no hindrance to nature.

I pass by and the old men bow,

As I bow, having surrendered essences

~Kokyo

When I Awake

When I awake,

It will not be to leave you

Rather, the game ended, in such a beginning

Since your eye lids fluttered

With your eyes raised ever so slightly

It will not suit to sleep in pain

However, the soil of slumber wetted,

Will turn to sand and be taken to the cultivated sea

Moreover, the sun will shine in my lidless eyes.

The Hound will slink away

And from the loft I will see you

Across the meadow, dancing

With undressed faces!

~Kokyo

When I was young,

I wished to walk on the clouds..

Now I am older,

And happy to view the sky from earth.

~Kokyo

My love,
I have cast your heart,
To the tortured lotus,
Out of my own perfidy -

And, though I search the pond,
My own heart is ever lost,

And will not be found again,
In this murky world!

~ Kokyo

Yellow Leaves

Thinking of my life, so far:

Leaves sodden, spent, sent

To swathe the trodden way.

Yellow they are, like certain apples,

Perhaps gold, or a wheel grinder's glints;

Hinting through deeds done,

That this is the day...

Who is coming?

Finds my leaves, sees how they mark the spot,

Soften the steps,

And hasten the journey's end...

Just as the shout, tinge, word, whisper;

Grin, scowl, blaze, glimmer;

Of an empty man,

Quickens all our hearts, and, it is hoped,

Allays all our pain...   ~Kokyo

Zazen

Sit, unwavering,

At the door of your heart,

Until it opens, softly, around you...

The sun is pouring;

The rain is shining –

The heart's adoring the world...

~Kokyo

Morning Moon

Do not disparage the morning moon –

That longing is its own fulfillment!

Full white winter disk,

Slipping into the hills

Carry my blessing to my Granddaughter...

~Papa Kokyo

For my Asian Ruby

When I had abandoned despair,

You entered,

And my heart began...

After almost thirty years –

Beached, salvaged; tempered, restored,

Ennobling our way –

We caress the soul of beauteous grace.

No one knows our heart's deep tinge;

No one can trace the glad shoots in our souls.

The lily of the valley you so adore,

Are nearly as graceful as our love.

And, this instant gone,

A tincture of our hearts, lingering,

Forever hues the dark night sky...   ~Kokyo

Emptiness

Camel pack on my desk

In its suchness

The cigarette I smoke

      And my tea

The doing in its vacuity

Yawning, this cold and lazy

        Winter morning

Climbing the steps in befuddled

Sleepy mind

The emptiness of this poem

~Kokyo

An Early Morning Parting

Gasping

Our ardent kiss,

We embraced in a field,

Amid a mild December's stubble;

I strode across the meadow

Knowing I would remember,

The blue tear on your lash,

And the pull of your eyes,

On my, suddenly, heavy shoulders.

~Kokyo

The Heart's Rain

Becoming broken,

I endured for many years –

Learning when to strive; when to yield.

After much travail,

My heart resonating deeply a tender resignation,

Resolutely, I walk further along;

The breezes awakening a joyful sigh _

What if it *should* rain!

~ Kokyo

And so it pleased you that I should be a worker in words;
Every experience you issued served to make me malleable to the craft -
Hardship wedded to enchantment was my spiritual sustenance;

You gave me the comfort of a beautiful Kwan Yin,
who watched on as I faltered; supporting as I felt my way along the crags
encouraging and admonishing;
forgiving the pain that a suffering soul seldom sees themselves inflict.

It pleased you to teach with pain; instruct with affliction.
To demand as the cornerstone of the temple you were secretly creating -
Faith!

A poet must not know the outcome of his instruction.
He must labor on in the darkest night, for one of time's eternities!

Then, it pleased you to build to the climax
where the poet recovers himself and his birthright...
slowly his friends and family gather at his inauguration....

And for space of time; he may freely ply his trade,
until the gift must in the finality be returned to emptiness...
where worlds of words issue forth

~ Kokyo

A Blanket of Snow

Sited out my window,

A late March snow has come:

The Buddhas are sending their Love...

~ Kokyo

I've lost your addled brain to noxious substances,
I know now I have; and, companion of my youth, my art (poetry),
is inadequate to assuage my weeping heart...

~Kokyo

Age

Winter splendour –

This aged vessel can no longer contain,

Its vision...

~Kokyo

Altar

How many times have I bowed before you;

Knelt,

And sat *Shikan Taza*?

Joy entering; abiding –

Resolving pain & conflict;

Restoring health and balance...

As Soyu Matsuoka Roshi, *O Sensei,* would often say:

"When you have *zazen*, you always have a place to go!"

Or, as Eihei Dogen called it:

"The Dharma Gate of Joyful Ease!"

Ho!

~ Kokyo

DharmaKaya

empty cavity,
inside to outside no discernible skin...
in this void, shelter, peace, love...
impossible to leave...

just, entrance obscured by illusory dust...

come back home...

wake up!

~ Kokyo

My Wife

I love it when I hear her say, rather imploringly –

"Dave"

I like it that she needs me...

I love to serve her.

She's got my back,

I'll return the favour by being her point man.

Each day with her, is a new discovery of bliss,

As we forge the possibilities of creative accord...

Completing the vows of commitment,

Having swum the perilous seas to harmonious concord;

And, leapt free of destructive strife...

~ Kokyo

Breezes blow across my garden,
idle days piled upon idle days without regrets...
adding to the Idyll of my latter years...
what I paid in rigorous dues,
have returned dividends in poetry beauty, family, contentment and Joy...

please understand my dear friends that nothing -
not even bleakness - remains forever without change

~ Kokyo

If it rains,

Eventually the air will clear...

It is that time that I will sing about...

For you, it may be always raining,

For me it was once too...

But, please remember, the clouds which darken your skies now

Eventually exhaust themselves,

And then the sun will sing rapturously through...

Don't despair, with downcast eyes,

But wait for waiting brings out the gladness of the sun...

And you know the sun shines, eventually, on everyone!

~ Kokyo

For Ruby Young

Have I journeyed this twisting mountain stream,
to be united at last with you on these shady river grasses...

~ Kokyo

Garden glorious -
prospect diminished...
flowers blooming from previous tillage...

spring planting...summer blooming...autumn demise...
winter....the vastness...

felt to be 'eternal, joyous selfless, pure!'

~ Kokyo

had a walk,
took some tea...
had a talk,
took a tree!

~ Kokyo

Heart Hunger

Eat up that living menu...

Family, friends, health professionals –

Entering the next faltering, courageous stage...

What will it be?

Struggle or renewed vigor;

Invalid, convalescence, and retirement from labor;

It will be the next phase,

Pregnant with new discoveries and fecund fruition...

Echoing onward into the sky!

~ Kokyo

I am old

My heart harbours no resentments;

But it is old also –

It drags me down...

But now see how my family flourishes...

~Kokyo

I follow my own *weird* –

I always prefer the 'before' pictures...

I like the books, 'in disfavour';

I went my own way;

I applied my own, unorthodox, methods...

(My shrewd grandmother pronounced me

'*Independent*' ;)

I have practiced on my own

Cultivated my own Self;

Devised my own recipes*!* ☺

But I invite you *all* to dine with me...

At my, **Peculiar Banquet of the Seasons**!

~Kokyo

I Forgot Whether I Bowed Just Now

Mold the passing temporalities;

Sketch the arising moment –

Turning the head in the next direction

Watching the flow of the stream, ride the craft home!

Gathering impressions,

Make, of morning, a meal;

Your promptings leading you on your way.

Obstacles becoming stumbling blocks;

We turn them into stepping stones.

At noon, stop and take direction,

Advancing where your foot falls.

Soon the magic of the day impresses;

As we wander all afternoon alone.

In the evening, codify,

And Master the meandering Way.

I Forgot Whether I Bowed Just Now

Intermediary:

The Teleology of a Life

Notes for '*Major Poem*' the twelve causal links. *Twelvefold chain of causation.*

How undercurrents throw up to the surface; causing affinities & events;
causing couples to unite and people to interact; leading the way of the
undercurrents to completion...then step off and back on, onward to the
endless Buddha path!

Undulating wordless mindings, and empty void, Buddha Womb

Motivating self to action...meetings move to affinities;

As relationships form.

Multifarious conjunctions must occur,

Timing events to tipping points ...merging undercurrents of the void –

Emptying to completion...then, step off...

Walking the endless Buddha Way...

I Forgot Whether I Bowed Just Now

I Forgot Whether I Bowed Just Now

...we suffer...we move to relief...life unfolds...

We are free...we move to suffer with (for) others...Bodhisattva Way!

_____

_____

(I met an injured Dove, who mended me – and took me home...

We lived on a crag, enduring many storms;

Wracked was our way;

Threatening wreckage on every turn.)

I fixed my craft fighting for the right to write;

Flourishing at separate points –

Becoming a legacy of Joy...

I Forgot Whether I Bowed Just Now

Denouement:

These latter days, I feel the strength, yet falter often...

My family & friends giving satisfying Joy...

Gladness gathers, resonating all over my heart!

I am thankful for a poetic life!

~ Kokyo 20 December 2013

Ideal Life

How would I like to have spent my life?

As I have, with you!

~ David

Kokyo Dharma

Break into Absolute Beauty

Dwelling there for eternity;

Turning stumbling blocks into stepping stones!

~ Kokyo

Mondo

Sensei Taiun (while lecturing on Art & Zen):

"Often art is created following on a 'happy accident'."

Kokyo (thinking of his father's fatal car accident):

"What about the unhappy accidents?"

Sensei Taiun: "There are none!"

Kokyo: (Smiles)

~Kokyo

My Wife

I love it when I hear her say, rather imploringly –

"Dave"

I like it that she needs me...

I love to serve her.

She's got my back,

I'll return the favor by being her point man.

Each day with her, is a new discovery of bliss,

As we forge the possibilities of creative accord...

Completing the vows of commitment,

Having swum the perilous seas to harmonious concord;

And, leapt free of destructive strife...

~ Kokyo

New Poem

The Love we bear our loved ones,

After Death –

Is Palpable!

~ Kokyo

December 23, 2013

New Poetics

Loose my tongue

So that I might drool droplets of cherry words;

Evergreen ferns of verse issuing from my pours,

Into an ocean of fishes of fiction and prawns of poetry!

~ Kokyo

Newly fallen snow,

Refreshing the earth...

Barren fields for so long,

In our Youth...

In Age, this newly fallen snow,

In Winter, we may consolidate,

& Return our Joy to the earth...

Flowering Spring!

~ Kokyo

Prescription for Flying-Ants (circa 1967)

(Recalled fragments of two very early poems combined into one, 2014)

An owl-eyed man sitting in judgment on his felt covered chair.

(Did the ticket-taker's expression have any content, or was it void?)

The flying-ants are out today!

(Did you know you had a body in your closet?)

Why, where are we going?

(We are going to Madame Tussauds')

~Kokyo

Rain of Love

(For Ruby)

I have asked much of you –

You have given more.

I have been a complex man

Requiring adjustments of Tolerance and Patience.

Perhaps I could have been kinder –

But I don't know how –

I have tried so hard.

Am I flawed? Yes.

I know I love you strong,

Like an Iron Rod.

Perhaps that was enough,

For you have returned it with a devotion, unflagging,

Like a Rain of Love.

(12/18/2013 1:19:10 AM   ~ Dave

River

I remember when I sat on Quam's porch,

After you ran from our meeting -

You were waiting for the end, like Wotan;

While I was lower than I've ever been,

But still confident of our outcome,

Hearing for the first time, River of Tears, by Clapton -

Today, from this prospect I see wide and far below...

Sky above, blue, and friends & family returning home:

I thank God for the healing practice of Poetry...

As it enter our lives leaving us devastated with Joy!

~ Kokyo

Ruby Young

I don't need to hold you;
I don't need to kiss you -
I just need to have you in our home,
Knowing, as I do, that you haven't dismissed me from your heart!

~ Kokyo David Young

Saving All Sentient Beings

We must countenance a world rife with sorrow -

emptying our hearts' wishes into the Void.

aspirations, daily kindnesses;

putting off hankering; can we put on splendour...

hurtling headlong; shucking our bodies off

gaining the heartland:

energy energy energy

until it no longer matters!

~Kokyo

Smoldering Birds

Swatting smoldering birds in pine branches;

Back yard activity –

The creation of poetry!

~ Kokyo

The first refreshing breezes,
in advance of Autumn -
may they be an emblem,

for lives, newly restored!

~ Kokyo

Poem *

Waiting as we used to wait for you two:

Deep sadness!

~ Kokyo   *for Shannon & James

Winter Storm Buddha

What presentiments inhabit the *Winter Wind*?

(Its intensity heard, as high in the trees it roars.)

When will our lessons be learned?

When will our efforts be returned?

We have crossed the droughts of Summer;

And hastened the repletion of Fall –

But, what will be the import of Winter –

And when will we end our song?

~ Kokyo

A Gift for Emily

Within this empty heart,

Grasping at nothing, you are contained...

At your birth, you entered, healing me,

As the 'girl of seven', spoken of in Buddhist Sutras,

You taught even this old man, enlarging his mind,

Teaching him to embrace the world, watching & blessing...

He has cared for you and loved

So much so that now he is full of you;

We have found our family together on this lonely plain

And do not fear that, at last,

Body dropping off...

This heart remains with you.

At last, body dropping of, this heart remains with you...

~ Papa Kokyo Tuesday, January 15, 2013

For Ruby

I've cared for you for forty years,

carrying your sorrows secretly in my heart...

When you faltered, I deferred,

you insisting upon up-righting yourself.

I wept inwardly as I watched your heart sorrow,

for you disallow displays...

Your heart has been vibrant - though unspoken,

it's beating was apparent...

you have filled me, you have thrilled me -

if I have fulfilled the mandate of our marriage

it was with a silent gift of salient, watchful understanding...

as you have done the same!

~ Kokyo Dave

Iya

My wife's nephew,

As he is a skilled horticulturalist, and kind friend,

Comes in the cultivating season

Helping me with my gardening,

(His daughter says he likes to work his grandfather's soil,

As I live on that great man's land.)

In the evening, we sit with my wife, in this garden

Drinking tea and talking with the neighbours,

Who come to share our Joy.

In winter, in our home, he is a regular guest,

Where we speak of philosophy, poetry and religion...

While enjoying a goblet of wine.

A teacher and a scholar –

He has become the conduit between the past & the future,

Unearthing knowledge like truffles to a boar.

I rejoice in my kinship with his fine family,

Sheltered in the cooling shade of an age distant oak tree.

A royal line, which even onto this day

Reflects it's ancient, noble splendour...

~ Kokyo David Young February 8, 2013

Kwan Yin watching

over white flower dying...

a simple, gentle Joy.

~ Kokyo

New Wine/Old Skins

An edifice has arisen,

In a place of exhibition –

My dwelling,

Wherein my family can reside...

All fixed, repaired –

Running smoothly

For the first time:

'Rapture spiritual beyond spiritual'

The wisps emitting a new Joy!

~ Kokyo

Out to Pasture

This poet's head is clouded once again,

And the same old people deride my mind's poor plight.

But they don't know that I've fulfilled my mandate,

And that the days that remain are for pasturing, and grazing –

They will be lucky to enjoy the milk of this tired, addled brain...mind the cud!

~ Kokyo

Savory Days

I know what a poet is:

Dwelling lovingly, he has his say –

Words falling here

          & there...

Empty, he finds his Kwan Yins

Suffering unto savory days,

Turning stumbling blocks into stepping stones...

Until, finally, body dropping off –

Last weary expressions,

Empty, with alacrity into Joyous, Awakened Heart!

~ Kokyo

Saying '*IT*'

For Sensei-san Taiun who admonished me:

"*If the Kokyo doesn't say it, it won't get said.*"

There is a Beauty entering and cavorting with the world.

Emptying ourselves, this Beauty fills our cavity, the *heart*

Sweeping the minds dusty floor –

Skipping like stones over a lake.

Sing with this heart,

Sit with this heart,

Die to this heart!

~Kokyo

So Long, Ariel, It's been good to Know Ya

From Tao Ch'ien through to Ryokan,

I've sung you, blithe one,

Off you go, find some other sucker...

Seriously, you've given me Joy of Joy –

Costing my mind,

Delivering me to Paradise on Alfred Street.

Your next should be stout of heart

Ready to endure all, to rise any given night at your becoming,

Without complaint and, mind the simpering

Thanks for the ride:

It's been fun chum, it's been swell pal

Unlike Prospero, you commanded me...

I went along for the ride _

Now, Piss off!

~ Kokyo January 26th/2012

The Odd Fellows Have Fallen

The Zendo is dimly lit; the monks are on morning Kinhin.

My nephew knows now – a spilt drop of tea doesn't matter:

The odd fellows have fallen...

Yesterday there was still time, now the meter has run out –

Tomorrow the edifice will crumble, and Papa will be silent.

But, for now there is time to drink Green Tea,

Talking of Lao Tzu & Buddha, the ole farts,

Tripling merrily on the brink of eternity.

On the verge of the Void the frozen landscape is melting,

And others will know the pleasures of poetry,

The passions of paucity.

Let them not say it has not been difficult...

Let them not say it has not been a Joy.

~ Kokyo January 28, 2013

Ageing

When I was young -
a short time ago -
I moved freely and talked to the folks in my daily round...
Young girls smiled at me and I chatted with strangers easily.

Now I am old and stiff -
I drag my foot...
folks don't stop to talk,
and the pretty girls no longer smile...

but my wife is kind...she still laughs with me and smiles gaily...

So she helps me face the coming chill.

~ Kokyo

You were gentle, you were kind;

You smiled every time we met.

I remember now,

It's your birthday today –

You were my mother.

~ Kokyo

Tara's Craft

Tara built a raft,

A craft for ferrying

The disenchanted, disillusioned,

Safety, deftly to the other shore.

With love, she hewed it with fine logs of solid oak,

With the skill of a crafts woman, and the toiling hands of a saint...

She bound the logs with compassionate tears,

And gentle glances of loving grace.

If you are wasted or disconsolate,

Ask for Tara's skillful means.

In her kindness, in her mercy,

She'll ferry you across this cruelty ravished plain.

You can still catch Tara's ferry,

It leaves each time she hears the wretched cry -

For, though you pay the fare in sorrow,

Its purchase yields Absolute Beauty and Perfect Joy!

~ Kokyo August 23rd 2015

Kokyo David Edgar Young

Pity the Tired Poet

Pity the tired poet,

He ravished his mind for poems;

Gathered from devastated experience.

Give him grace till the end of his days,

To live them in his garden of verdant words.

Grant him rest and Joy, while he lingers,

Here on the rine of life,

Deprived of strength, loved by his family -

Emptied of impediment,

Released, acquiesced, and at home.

~ Kokyo May 16th 2016

Poem for a Sick Friend

We found you smiling,

And strangely serene today,

My dear friend;

A new resignation and acceptance

Shone on your wizened face...

There is a Comfort,

Which comes after great travail,

To those whose hearts are good.

~ Kokyo

Kokyo David Edgar Young

For Lee (my niece)

As you wished,

Lilacs bud.

By the time you arrive,

They will be long gone,

The Summer will be spent -

Only to be revived by you!

~ Uncle David

Accomplishment

I planted, and grew a beautiful Azalia -

Now the bees gather honey from it -

Poetry is the same!

~ Kokyo

Death

(a scary poem)

Somewhere, anytime, a door will bang!

Nature is in a state of uncertainty,

As with conditions,

Flux, is the way of the world...

A door bangs -

Sometimes it will open,

At such times,

Be prepared to jump right in!

~ Kokyo may 26th 2016

Kokyo David Edgar Young

I Do not Want to Loose the Nuances

I do not want to looose the nuances,

Of the impressions,

(Or how they will appear in an,

Index of First Lines)

Whether it is a bogus poem,

The reader may decide,

For now, it I enough,

To return to sleep,

To the magnificent dreams,

Which engendered these few lines...

~ Kokyo May 26th 2016

The garden I've created,

Will thrive after I am gone:

My shrubs will gratify others esthetic sense...

So my poems will please others,

Having a life of their own,

In many times, in many places...

Sur gut!

~ Kokyo May 21st 2016

Ask the henchwoman to delay her approach -

We can stay a little longer in the mist of decay...

As I shift my body about yearning to attain sleep

So my heart learns to long for death.

The witch of wakefulness cries, "Arise and be about your chosen craft!

The spring of poetry seeps up through the soil,

And you must savor the spices of ageing observance. "_____"

Don't try to squeeze the exquisite clouds of experience -Let them infuse the void.

That summer's garment was so delicate,

The tender texture of the air around you -

~ Kokyo

Kokyo David Edgar Young

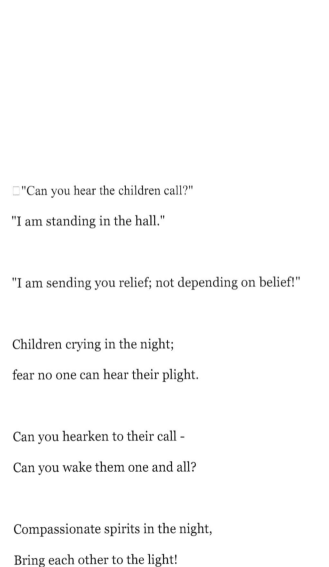

"Can you hear the children call?"

"I am standing in the hall."

"I am sending you relief; not depending on belief!"

Children crying in the night;
fear no one can hear their plight.

Can you hearken to their call -
Can you wake them one and all?

Compassionate spirits in the night,
Bring each other to the light!

~ Kokyo September 2nd/2015

Kokyo David Edgar Young

Reflecting on My Poem *'After the Rain'*

Only I know

What it is to have written,

'After the Rain'.

Forty-one years later,

I remember the conception of;

'except as much as would lead you consider,

the freshness left by the rain!'

I only

Will ever have this memory!

~ Kokyo

Morning Moon

Do not disparage the morning moon –

That longing is its own fulfillment!

Full white winter disk,

Slipping into the hills

Carry my blessing to my Granddaughter...

~ David Young (Feb. 24/05)

Lilies of the Valley

(*"Consider the lilies of the field; they neither reap neither do they sow....But I tell you that even Solomon, in all his splendor, was not arrayed as one of these"*

~ **Jesus' Sermon on the Mount)**

So we began our marriage, obeying in simplicity,

The injunctions on worry from *The Sermon on the Mount*;

We have traveled far "looking to god for all things";

Our end-journey will surely be peaceful and complete –

I remember seeing you at the IGA, such a flower,

So arrayed as a Lilly-of-the-Valley...

You took my breath away...

And when you said I could call, my springtime opened.

Lilies 2)

Without you my life would be dust; dry impalpable dust;

With you: enchanting in a tender numinous manner.

Evening's lucidity refines the love as it has finally grown,

As a brook recalls us to our own heart;

Our union, our family, as my life reaches its zenith,

Is a charm which I will bring into the eternal;

And the love with which we have covered all our doings;

Will remain as the butterflies remain...

In our hearts; in Emily's & Shawn's & Karen's,

And all we have touched.

~ David

That Night in August,

With you on the cottage dirt roads,

After the party; when the moon was full;

And the leaves quivered with youthful freshness

And you were so warm in my arms;

And music was new; and we, delicate, holding each other

We kissed; we were so young and new;

And your lips trembled and were tasty like I could never describe;

...

And then our Love lost its balance so hard and we were alone;

And empty...so empty...

And suffering introduced itself to me and I never felt better;

Until I met *the one* who would teach me to *rejoice* each day;

As though Joy might go out of stock;

So we had better spend it today...

For tomorrow   **~ Kokyo**

A Poem Especially for You

As evening settles in, I find

This afternoon's restlessness gone...

Resignation is my policy now –

I have shrugged off my rancour;

And, turning homeward,

I stroll at a relaxed but tired pace,

Under the kind eye of the yellow, watchful moon.

-David Young

Kokyo sits zazen on Fitzpatrick Mountain,

Below him three counties in view –

Is it world-weariness or Compassion,

Which whitens his bones and turns them to dust?

Or is he just an arthritic, old fart! ☺

~Kokyo

Polish

There are those who,

living 400 miles away,

dwell here in my heart.

Old friends pass my home,

pursuing their careers;

They have their satisfactions –

I have poetry,

and the hardships of true living...

Joys gather around my heart,

as the one who has climbed these years with me –

steadfast, devoted, weakened –

proffers her cheek in her alluring manner;

then polishes our sparse silver,

as she has polished our marriage

all these long, rich, full years...

David Young

\

Life's Predicament

Young girl,

On foot along the path...

Blown beyond her pace by stiff winds –

Hopefully she soon regains her poise!

~ Kokyo

Lilies

A yellow & a purple Iris –

Beautifully iridescent against the sun...

Over time, ravishing storms devastate our delicate flowers...

Poisonous, they lay lifeless on the garden bed...

~ Kokyo

Sound Love

Tears fell,

As I watched you boarding,

Your rotting dory, up stream,

On the river of Despair.

Hurriedly, I ran ahead,

Downstream,

Cutting my skin on glass and brambles.

Now I sit, assuredly, at the mouth,

Waiting to cast the net of my Love,

Snatching you from the ocean of Oblivion

Knowing that Love, true and full,

Does not fail to rescue us from,

Despair.

David Young

"One Happiness Scatters a Thousand Sorrows"*

Because I have been Joyful and bright,

Has your way been lightened?

Have you been happier since I was here?

And may I rejoice that I have been effective,

In my mission to alleviate your Pain?

As long as your path has been smoother and easier;

And your joys more plentiful,

I may hope to have had a part in easing your struggles;

And I may rest, knowing, you are certain in your steps,

And lastingly steadied in your course, because of me!

~ Kokyo

Why Does the Laughing Buddha Laugh?

Because Joy

Trumps

Sorrow

Because suffering

Is apparent...

And serenity

Sits sure and certain!

~ Kokyo

Joy

Gleeful Joy

Mad Joy –

 Bounding over the hills Joy...

Compassionate Joy,

Skillful Joy –

Bringing them home for dinner Joy!

When you see the end Joy;

When you're lost in the darkness Joy;

Joy when you leap at the sight of your long lost home

Stumbling with Joy over the hillocks;

Panting for the breath of your wife on your Joy stained face Joy!

~ Kokyo

Love

Love audaciously

Ride the exquisite horse of love with valor,

Give her rein; use the stirrup, never the whip.

Risk the hurdles; finish the course

Gather the garland

Putting love foremost, sacrifice all;

Should you fall, never regret mounting,

Never decline the chase!

David Young

Suffering/Joy

Sun seared, wind wasted,

Having assayed the depths of suffering-

Everything is always alright!

Suffering is efficacious –

Leading to fulfillment:

Without travel, there is no destination:

No walking, no arriving...

Dark night

Suddenly – moon no longer obscured:

Liberating beauty abounding!

Trees sing with the breeze

The broken-hearted lift their eyes,

Seeking relief;

As compassion seeps up, softly,

Through the evening air-

So we sing, causing no harm.

David Young

Second & Third Noble Truths

(After Buddha)

Craving

Desirable states of mind/body/estate,

We are unhappy...

Not craving

Desirable states of mind/body/estate,

We are happy!

~ Kokyo

Seasons

All over the province
rain & freezing rain

in my heart
this mossy peace
as I sit Zazen
with Bella, the Maltese/Shiatsu

Caring joyfully and compassionately
for all I've found...
may they see the fruition of their sorrow;
the end of their journey;
and the realization of their Joy.

Spring is late in coming...
it holds off ('till we are all gathered?)

But, eventually it comes
and we laugh in the warm evening breezes of summer!

~ Kokyo

A Gift for Emily

Within this empty heart,

Grasping at nothing, you are contained...

At your birth, you entered, healing me,

As the 'girl of seven', spoken of in Buddhist Sutras,

You taught even this old man, enlarging his mind,

Teaching him to embrace the world, watching & blessing...

He has cared for you and loved

So much so that now he is full of you;

We have found our family together on this lonely plain

And do not fear that, at last,

Body dropping off...

This heart remains with you.

~ Papa Kokyo Tuesday, January 15, 2013

For Ruby

I've cared for you for forty years,
carrying your sorrows secretly in my heart...

When you faltered, I deferred,
you insisting upon up-righting yourself.

I wept inwardly as I watched your heart sorrow,
for you disallow displays...

Your heart has been vibrant - though unspoken,
it's beating was apparent...

you have filled me, you have thrilled me -

if I have fulfilled the mandate of our marriage
it was with a silent gift of salient, watchful understanding...

as you have done the same!

~ Kokyo Dave

Iya

My wife's nephew,

As he is a skilled horticulturalist, and kind friend,

Comes in the cultivating season

Helping me with my gardening,

(His daughter says he likes to work his grandfather's soil,

As I live on that great man's land.)

In the evening, we sit with my wife, in this garden

Drinking tea and talking with the neighbors,

Who come to share our Joy.

In winter, in our home, he is a regular guest,

Where we speak of philosophy, poetry and religion...

While enjoying a goblet of wine.

A teacher and a scholar –

He has become the conduit between the past & the future,

Unearthing knowledge like truffles to a boar.

I rejoice in my kinship with his fine family,

Sheltered in the cooling shade of an age distant oak tree.

A royal line, which even onto this day

Reflects it's ancient, noble splendour...

~ Kokyo David Young February 8, 2013

Kwan Yin watching

over white flower dying...

a simple, gentle Joy.

~ Kokyo

A Nobel Truth

All over the world,

So many heartaches –

All because of someone else!

~ Kokyo

A Farewell in Courage and Gratitude

And I knew all the sorrows of the human heart;

All its Joys were given me in recompense.

In literature and philosophy I found the image of my experience,

And was given courage and recognition of my ways.

Mine it was to suffer with; to gather the lost together;

To position the sorrowful in the light;

And send the bitter into understanding.

To give them the courage and appreciation of their ways.

And now, gathered, as we are, on evening's shore;

Preparing to depart; may we touch in identification;

May our waning be our fulfillment;

And may we gain in courage and gratitude, for our way.

~ Kokyo

A Blanket of Snow

A late March snow has come:

The Buddhas are sending their Love...

~ Kokyo

A Profound Poem

Taking no deliberate action:

Following the promptings,

Find your way home...

One of your *forget-me-nots*

Tumbling out of your hands –

Let it, unhindered,

Find its way where it falls...

Perhaps you will see it no more –

It is no longer in your hands!

~ Kokyo

A Surrealistic Remedy

A white eye-ball,

Pierced by a timber pier;

Is foreman to the reconstruction of my soul...

Under an egg-yolk sun,

My senses saw & hammer daily;

Blending my soul in wedlock,

To their objects.

Launched, it bobs upon the sea of my awareness;

Anchored firmly to my testicals,

Its becomes the conjunction between my toes,

And my coffee mug!

~ David Young (circa 1967 – recalled in its entirety 2014

Agape

Quietly sitting in meditation,

Surveying the graying sky:

A bird flies across the clouds,

While love springs from my heart

Emptying into the earth and heavens —

As my friend Shannon

Elicits a love leaping out,

Protecting - heartening her!

~ David Young

All Those Horrid Years,

When blood flowed like molten lead through my stinging brain;

And it stank, like a stagnant thing, like a withered leaf.

I reached up for things just beyond my reach;

And cried out in voiceless shrieks;

But the harsh desert sand, in my mouth, was the only stark reply.

It is then I learned to sing; to, as I say, *rejoice...*

And **she** helped me, the *Red Jewel,*

The one who spoke in smooth silk; and covered my pain with balm.

It was a stark way fraught with Pain;

It was a pure way which taught Joy, without stain...

~ Kokyo

As I Live my Life for You

I give you all my strength,

Unstintingly,

As I live my life for you.

I devise skillful means

To alleviate your pain;

As I live my life for you.

I revive after exhausting

My reserves;

As I live my life for you.

It is my pleasure

To do all for you;

As I live my life for you.

When I have done,

And my life is spent –

I'll lay down my life for you.   ~ Kokyo

Cohabitating with Spiders

I cohabitate with the spiders,

They have free range in my home,

Despite my granddaughter's aversion.

However, should they frighten her –they face certain death!

~ Kokyo

Dara's Bling,

Like a Buddhist flag...

Stuck in the wind –

Flapping by itself!

~ Kokyo

Empathy

My granddaughter's sad, because she has no sibling;

My neighbor seems sad because she is alone;

The town is depressed because it has no industry...

And I turn to go to bed,

Sad, because I have no remedy for their woes.

~ Kokyo

For You

As long as you are sad,

I also am sad...

When you rejoice,

So also do I.

When you laugh & sing,

So also does my heart...

For I bear what you bear,

And I am there always with you!

~ Kokyo Papa

Foundation of Joy

Our hearts are settled on a foundation of Joy:

Though waves of sorrow often rock our boat,

The sea of our heart, allowed to return to calm,

Is grounded on a verdant seabed of Joy and Exultation!

Never losing site of this,

We can journey undulating oceans

Assured that the outcome of our, perhaps, arduous way will be...

Abundant Peace!

~ Kokyo

Fourth Nobel Truth

(Noble Eightfold Path ~ After Buddha)

Knowing Truth,

Thinking, Speaking Truthfully & Kindly,

Acting well...working as practice;

One goes on to Concentrate, Meditate...

Hence finds Wisdom –

This is the way to Liberation.

~ Kokyo

The Kokyo Touch

I reach here,

    I reach there...

All I touch turns to dust!

~Kokyo

In the utter acceptance –

Is the release!

~ Kokyo

Joy

Gleeful Joy

Mad Joy –

 Bounding over the hills Joy...

Compassionate Joy,

Skillful Joy –

Bringing them home for dinner Joy!

When you see the end Joy;

When you're lost in the darkness Joy;

Joy when you leap at the sight of your long lost home

Stumbling with Joy over the hillocks;

Panting for the breath of your wife on your Joy stained face Joy!

~ Kokyo

Kokyo sits zazen on Fitzpatrick Mountain,

Below him three counties in view –

Is it world-weariness or Compassion,

Which whitens his bones and turns them to dust?

Or is he just an old fart! ☺

~Kokyo

Life's Predicament

Young girl,

On foot along the path...

Blown beyond her pace by stiff winds –

Hopefully she soon regains her poise!

~ Kokyo

Lilies of the Valley

("*Consider the lilies of the field; they neither reap neither do they sow....But I tell you that even Solomon, in all his splendor, was not arrayed as one of these*"

~ Jesus' Sermon on the Mount)

So we began our marriage, obeying in simplicity,

The injunctions on worry from *The Sermon on the Mount*;

We have traveled far "looking to god for all things";

Our end-journey will surely be peaceful and complete –

I remember seeing you at the IGA, such a flower,

So arrayed as a Lilly-of-the-Valley...

You took my breath away...

And when you said I could call, my springtime opened.

Lilies 2)

Without you my life would be dust; dry impalpable dust;

With you: enchanting in a tender numinous manner.

Evening's lucidity refines the love as it has finally grown,

As a brook recalls us to our own heart;

Our union, our family, as my life reaches its zenith,

Is a charm which I will bring into the eternal;

And the love with which we have covered all our doings;

Will remain as the butterflies remain...

In our hearts; in Emily's & Shawn's & Karen's,

And all we have touched.

~ David

Lilies

A yellow & a purple Iris –

Beautifully iridescent against the sun...

Over time, ravishing storms devastate our delicate flowers...

Poisonous, they lay lifeless on the garden bed...

~ Kokyo

Love's Emulsion

How long you've watched over my shoulder

Breathing your love into all I do.

My love deepens with all sorrow,

Your heart, there with me, shines and grieves.

Caring for your welfare – in daily life; at rest –

(And when do you ever rest, Ruby?)

Each morning agreeing to live another day,

Catching the glimmers of light shimmering on evening's harbor…

Till, passing joyously together into the sky,

Our hearts emptying into one emulsion of Love.

~ Kokyo David Young (circa 2004)

Moonlit Harbor

Sitting on this Rock

Throughout the Night –

This shimmering Moonlight!

~ Kokyo

My Poems Are My Children

My poems are my children;

Creating; nurturing; and setting them on their own:

Should they do well, become influential,

And establish a following;

Is largely dependent on the start in life

I am able to give to them;

How they were raised; and their constitutional nature...

May they all be of quality stock; and find their rightful

Place in the world!

~ Kokyo

Old age

Is not a time.

It is a condition

Of illness, decrepitude and decay.

The mountains have all been climbed;

The rivers forged, and the streams crossed...

If now, in my garden, in my Alfred Street Hermitage,

Strength gone,

Always falling, aching and sore,

Body in dissolution;

What does it matter...

The race is run; there is love in the heart;

Family flourishing –

And I am always rejoicing!

~ Kokyo

"One Happiness Scatters a Thousand Sorrows"*

Because I have been Joyful and bright,

Has your way been lightened?

Have you been happier since I was here?

And may I rejoice that I have been effective,

In my mission to alleviate your Pain?

As long as your path has been smoother and easier;

And your joys more plentiful,

I may hope to have had a part in easing your struggles;

And I may rest, knowing, you are certain in your steps,

And lastingly steadied in your course, because of me!

~ Kokyo

* Chinese proverb

Petals Falling

Taking no deliberate action:

Following the promptings,

Find your way home...

One of your *forget-me-nots*

Tumbling out of your hands –

Let it, unhindered,

Find its way where it falls...

Perhaps you will see it no more –

It is no longer in your hands!

~ Kokyo

A Poem Especially for You

As evening settles in, I find

This afternoon's restlessness gone...

Resignation is my policy now –

I have shrugged off my rancour;

And, turning homeward,

I stroll at a relaxed but tired pace,

Under the kind eye of the yellow, watchful moon.

-David Young

Poem for Pearl

('You should write a poem about Pearl' ~ Ruby)

Enlightened Christian, my Aunt...

The 'one true Pearl' who left us to journey to China,

Early in the twentieth century,

Staying for over forty years of service!

"Seek God in all things!" you taught...I listened!

You taught most effectively with your presence...

How I remember a drive with you, when, returning home,

You exclaimed: "I'll remember this drive as long as I live!"

- This went directly into my heart.

Ruby remembers you, in your eighties,

Skipping over puddles laughing like a school girl...

When we were first married, you visited,

Exclaiming, "Praise the lord!" after I smiled my Joy.

They tried to bury you alive – they tried to shoot you...

But they couldn't...

God wouldn't allow it!

Still I hear you in my heart... 'Dear David'

'Praise God for dear Ruby!'

"No mourning!'

I think of your saviors' words,

"With you I leave my peace!'

You have left yours fully with me and mine!

~ Kokyo David Edgar Young

Reflecting on My Poem *'After the Rain'*

Only I know

What it is to have written,

'After the Rain'.

Forty-one years later,

I remember the conception of;

'except as much as would lead you consider,

the freshness left by the rain!'

I only

Will ever have this memory!

~ Kokyo

Ruby Came as the Night Departed –

Stirring the emergence of stunning day.

She stayed as we learned to cherish gladness;

And sustain the heightening allure ...

We studied each lesson thoroughly;

Asking only for the bloom of each new day -

     Storm; Drought or Harvest.

In Darkness we kept faith;

In Sheer day – we entered the territory...

And abolished study...

Today, our seasons arrive and depart;

We react to each in the appropriate manner...

No more, the resistance; no longer, the pestilence.

~ Kokyo

Seasons

All over the province
rain & freezing rain

in my heart
this mossy peace
as I sit Zazen
with Bella, the Maltese/Shiatsu

Caring joyfully and compassionately
for all I've found...
may they see the fruition of their sorrow;
the end of their journey;
and the realization of their Joy.

Spring is late in coming...
it holds off ('till we are all gathered?)

But, eventually it comes
and we laugh in the warm evening breezes of summer!

~ Kokyo

Second & Third Noble Truths

(After Buddha)

Craving

Desirable states of mind/body/estate,

We are unhappy...

Not craving

Desirable states of mind/body/estate,

We are happy!

~ Kokyo

"Shining Brighter Until the Perfect Day"

Practice continues, perhaps intensifies,

(Although aging is a decline which must be accepted)

And each day is a glory in the decline;

Full of abiding discoveries, deepening, ripening –

Relenting; renouncing that which must fall away;

Opening to the expanse of the Buddha Womb...

The DarmaKaya where all resolves into Serenity;

"Eternal, Joyous Selfless, Pure!"

Accept, Rejoice, Release...

~ Kokyo

Sitting

Sore ass

Green tea & honey

Joy Unbounded!

~ Kokyo

That night in August,

With you on the cottage dirt roads,

After the party; when the moon was full;

And the leaves quivered with youthful freshness

And you were so warm in my arms;

And music was new; and we, delicate, holding each other

We kissed; we were so young and new;

And your lips trembled and were tasty like I could never describe;

...

And then our Love lost its balance so hard and we were alone;

And empty...so empty...

And suffering introduced itself to me and I never felt better;

Until I met *the one* who would teach me to *rejoice* each day;

As thought Joy might go out of stock;

So we had better spend it today...

For tomorrow...   **~ Kokyo**

That same

"Still Small Voice"/"True Man of no Rank"

Is Buddha, is God...

This is a revelation/realization

Of which I am certain.

~ Kokyo

The Dissolution of the Poet

"I once was intelligent", or so my story goes;

But ill health and over use of the brain;

Coupled with trying experiences –

Issue: an stupid old man!

~ Kokyo

"The Sun whose Rays..."*

One may be confident without being haughty;

Self-assured, but not vain...

We might be humble, yet aware of our capabilities.

The sun shines warmly and lovingly,

Yet she does not begrudge her life giving light...

She lends her light to the moon,

Flirts with him,

But is ever faithful and constant;

She will endure... She will endure... She will endure...

~ Kokyo (Thursday, January 30, 2014)

Title, *Yum Yum's* Aria from *The Mikado* of Gilbert & Sullivan

This temple

Cavity of my awareness –

As the clouds drift off,

The sun streams in…

~ Kokyo

This temple

Cavity of my awareness –

As the clouds drift off,

The sun streams in…

~ Kokyo

Weakening Blows

One of Shakespeare's 'thousand natural shocks'

Occurring suddenly –

Constitution weakened, anything could happen…

Coming days a hazard:

Zazen through the night –

I am ready.

~ Kokyo

Why Does the Laughing Buddha Laugh?

Because Joy

Trumps

Sorrow

Because suffering

Is apparent...

And serenity

Sits sure and certain!

~ Kokyo

Your Tree

I'm sorry I cut your tree down.

On an impulse I cut it down thinking it spoiled the garden.

I didn't realize it meant so much to you;

But I should have known,

Remembering how often we played tag around it.

And when you saw that it was gone;

You became so angry with me...

I am sorry I cut your favorite tree down,

For now, as you are growing older;

I have only the stump to remind me of my betrayal!

~ Kokyo

Lost in the Buddha way,

I don't know where I am...

But, home is all around!

~ Kokyo

I Lived for Forty Years in a House Lined with Poetry

I lived for forty years in a house lined with Poetry,

With an exquisitely beautiful Bodhisattva of Compassion.

We raised a carpenter, who built us a temple,

With a Green Tara in the altar room.

Sheltered by their graceful personal beauty,

Forbearing long...until our faltering steps became certain,

We then began to lead others of the long, arduous journey

Home, to a house lined with Poetry.

~ Kokyo David Young,

On the occasion of forty years marriage to the splendid

Ruby Wong Young

Accomplishment

I planted, and grew a beautiful Azalia -

Now the bees gather honey from it -

Poetry is the same!

~ Kokyo

Ancient Body Dust

Sweet conversations, sweet affirmations -

I'd truly say, that you take after me!

Dusk of morning, oil freight leaving town,

In grey sky and dirty brown earth -

One light only besides mine.

Beauty hides in the harshness of things -

Tumbling along on this ruddy dirt ball -

It is only during and after passage through torrents,

That the glassy smooth harbour is achieved...

You where there, you have seen,

I cannot say I would be here, 'cept for you.

In this dawning of never ending day,

Join me as I dwell, joyful, in my tawny garden.

~ Kokyo

☐ "Can you hear the children call?"

"I am standing in the hall."

"I am sending you relief; not depending on belief!"

Children crying in the night;

fear no one can hear their plight.

Can you hearken to their call -

Can you wake them one and all?

Compassionate spirits in the night,

Bring each other to the light!

~ Kokyo September 2nd/2015

Kokyo David Edgar Young

Death

(a scary poem)

Somewhere, anytime, a door will bang!

Nature is in a state of uncertainty,

As with conditions,

Flux, is the way of the world...

A door bangs -

Sometimes it will open,

At such times,

Be prepared to jump right in!

~ Kokyo may 26th 2016

Dinner with the Darryl Wongs

Rather than vociferous song,

or an evening of wild dance and wine...

to be sheltered form the storm once again by your family,

in a dinner with quiet, gentle conversation,

warmly appreciative of each other...

this is the true kinship!

~ Kokyo

Kokyo David Edgar Young

For Lee (my niece)

As you wished,

Lilacs bud.

By the time you arrive,

They will be long gone,

The Summer will be spent -

Only to be revived by you!

~ Uncle David

Ask the henchwoman to delay her approach -

We can stay a little longer in the mist of decay...

As I shift my body about yearning to attain sleep

So my heart learns to long for death.

The witch of wakefulness cries, "Arise and be about your chosen craft!

The spring of poetry seeps up through the soil,

And you must savor the spices of ageing observance. "_____"

Don't try to squeeze the exquisite clouds of experience -Let them infuse the void.

That summer's garment was so delicate,

The tender texture of the air around you -

~ Kokyo

Thanks It gurgles up in the mountain springs, a life,

Frolicking in the verdant undergrowth of youth...

Hitting the streams it gurgles with delight;

Then unfortunately the difficult rapids, winding the river,

Seeking ever, the ocean, rescinding the ragged life....

Findng, at last, the full and silent ocean,

Eternal, Joyous, Selfless, Pure...

~ Kokyo

Thanks I Do not Want to Lose the Nuances

I do not want to lose the nuances, Of the impressions,

(Or how they will appear in an, Index of First Lines)

Whether it is a bogus poem, The reader may decide,

For now, it I enough, To return to sleep,

To the magnificent dreams,

Which engendered these few lines...

~ Kokyo May 26th 2016

☐Pity the Tired Poet

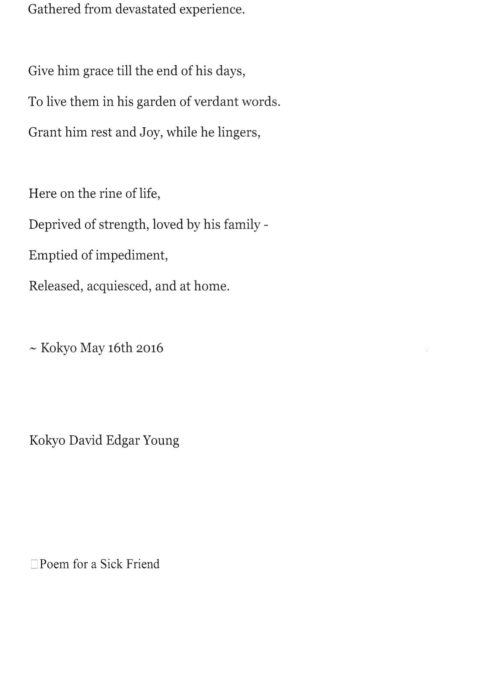

Pity the tired poet,

He ravished his mind for poems;

Gathered from devastated experience.

Give him grace till the end of his days,

To live them in his garden of verdant words.

Grant him rest and Joy, while he lingers,

Here on the rine of life,

Deprived of strength, loved by his family -

Emptied of impediment,

Released, acquiesced, and at home.

~ Kokyo May 16th 2016

Kokyo David Edgar Young

☐Poem for a Sick Friend

We found you smiling,

And strangely serene today,

My dear friend;

A new resignation and acceptance

Shone on your wizened face...

There is a Comfort,

Which comes after great travail,

To those whose hearts are good.

~ Kokyo

Kokyo David Edgar Young

Tara's Craft

Tara built a raft,

A craft for ferrying

The disenchanted, disillusioned,

Safety, deftly to the other shore.

With love, she hewed it with fine logs of solid oak,

With the skill of a crafts woman, and the toiling hands of a saint...

She bound the logs with compassionate tears,

And gentle glances of loving grace.

If you are wasted or disconsolate,

Ask for Tara's skillful means.

In her kindness, in her mercy,

She'll ferry you across this cruelty ravished plain.

You can still catch Tara's ferry,

It leaves each time she hears the wretched cry -

For, though you pay the fare in sorrow,

Its purchase yields Absolute Beauty and Perfect Joy!

~ Kokyo August 23rd 2015

Kokyo David Edgar Young

The garden I've created,

Will thrive after I am gone:

My shrubs will gratify others esthetic sense...

So my poems will please others,

Having a life of their own,

In many times, in many places...

Sur gut!

~ Kokyo May 21st 2016

I will Give you Poems

I will give you poems in season -

Be quick to catch the lines -

I counsel and deliver,

At sunset there are threads of whisperings,

At sunrise, a motion to dismiss,

Adjourn till dusk of a nearer night,

In your garden I lurk,

Capture the glimmers lying in wait.

Shed the shredded hurt and grasping -

"Empty yourself, that you might be filled."

~ Kokyo

Moonlight

Moonlight lites the wayfarer's way
Ever whispering of her destination...

In darkest night, lady moonlight,
Breaks from behind storm clouds -
Illuminating our nature, is her nature...

Making the path, the goal -
Traveling the way, is completeing the way.

~ Kokyo June 8th 2016

Nirvana

Eternal, joyous, intimate, pure

Body gone, mind gone

Eternal, joyous, intimate, pure

Sunshine has heightened my Joy;

And,with supplication,

Illumined my darkened paths...

Sunlight gladdens the heart,

and casts memories in bright relief -

But the dark is where the heart

Explores itself in evening's serenity,

And resolves a life in consolidation & release...

~ Kokyo June 8th 2016

This I have learned:

As I grow hoarse,

I, once more, try to achieve eloquent speech:

In our garden are dirt & crawley things -

Necessary for growth!

~ Kokyo June 9th 2016

Given the nature of her condition,

Much pain and sorrow was unavoidable.

We did the best we could,

Yet her suffering persisted...

Nothing could help, nothing,

Until he helped her gain a new foothold,

A footing based on acceptance & care...

He taught her aquesience,

Enabling the best self of both

To come to the forefront -

Establishing them on new ground,

Of relinquished demand,

And acquired diligence.

~ Kokyo

A New Poem for Shannon & James

If, "I die so that you might live",

Then your death has given new life to me;

For the release from your struggle, has released me,

Increased my strength, and delivered me to life.

It is Spring and gardening begins anew,

Both literally and figuratively;

I have tulips, daffodils, family and loved ones to nurture -

And may the world be my garden,

And my I deliver poems of mercy to the world's door;

As you two have, continually,

Brought biscuits and vegetables to ours!

~ Kokyo

After James & Shannon

Thrown off balance

By the loss of you;

We try to get ourselves to that centred place...

But only time will accomplish this...

And spring comes,

With zazen awakens my old heart...

You two have, at last, found rest;

Soon, hopefully, ours will be restored, as well.

~ Kokyo

Dragging this tired body on my morning round:

Groceries, a call at the hospital,

Lunch with a friend, then return home by bus...

Rest now, Smetana & Beethoven -

I find, despite aging, I get more pleasure out of living...

Mental health restored, physically okay -

Sun or shine, at least for a time, we'll be fine!

~ Kokyo

Blue Skies on the Western Horizon

Blue skies on the Western horizon -

Helicon days may return.

The storm has raged all through the endless, hopeless night.

The pain seemed never to end; the goul of illness prospered...

But through perseverance, dawn has come,

And now this distant blue promises renewal,

As all the sages of old promised.

And you who have journeyed through this night with me;

With me, shall roam this spreading garden!

~ Kokyo (a poem for Ruby on Mother's Day)

Dusk of a pleasant winter evening,

Preceeded by a peaceful afternoon -

Growing mossy in mind; as all is released to the void...

I wait on the cusp of the world, awaiting tea avec tu!

~ Kokyo

Fin Again

My light grows dim.

Someday will dawn & set without me.

I will be hiding in the all of it...

Seek me in the corners of your hearts.

~ Kokyo

Flowers Grow in Death Valley

A new Spring promises,

Can we melt our anger...

We have tarried long near the precipice,

 Will we, perhaps be plunged?

But can I see, in the bluelight of these dripping icicles,

A thaw in threatening calamity?

For, though all around seems precipitous -

Flowers grow in Death Valley!

~ Kokyo   Febuary 25th 2016

Gatha

A field of compassion,

Issues forth comfort to beings,

Suffering illness and calamity...

May those in need receive refuge and release.

~ Kokyo

Hymn

Dear Lord,

I am tired, and do thy comfort need;

Draw nigh, and let me come to thee...

I am sore; have suffered endlessly;

Let me die, and let me come to thee.

Ruby sunsets you have given me;

Let me linger, and enjoy them endlessly...

I rejoyce, on being grandfathered in;

Let me live; and enjoy this office given!

~ Kokyo

If you were no longer here

How would it be for you, my love,

If I were no longer there ?

Would you turn in the bed, feeling a gap,

A lack, a void, filled only by aching...

If you were conspicuously gone,

Would the silence yell, like the dead of winter -

Would my mind sound in a mute, constant screaming,

Would I turn in my pillow like the face of death?

My wife, one day one of we two will be suddenly absence,

And the finality, will deaden us into a numb despair,

Which can be filled only by the removal of the other,

In a reunion of serene, joyous, intimacy...

~ Kokyo

Mothers Flower Children

Sway of cherry bush giving pleasure -

Sun, bees - birds chirp;

Green Spring shoots from ruddy soil.

Daffodils for mothers -

Children flower earth!

Kokyo

New Poem

I, a remnant,

Sitting on the edge of creation,

Gathering poetic dust -

Shaking my clothing over the web -

Motes of words, thus scattered forward...

~ Kokyo

Pain

Body pain;

Mind suffering -

Bodhisattva agony,

The world's sorrow...

Our woes are the woes of all;

And, if we suffer, we suffer for,

And in relation to every being...

Our travail does not isolate us -

It unites us!

~ Kokyo

Poem of Joy

(Forsythia; Cherry Bush; Dappled Willow)

This garden embraces me,

I grow in it;

It cousins my heart!

This garden is my heart; this heart, my garden...

With my loved ones firmly planted in.

Fertilize my garden with my heart;

The earth, my heart may flower,

Upward to the empty sky!

~ Kokyo

Writing poems that will warm the world...(fragment of a prayer)

I am crouched in the crevices of the World's Garden...

I am cousin to the secret whisperings of the heart...

I wait by the gate...

I offer you the honeyed way...

I invite you to my table...I render you your gathered garlands...

I enable the writing of poems to warm the world...

I usher in the era of effortless agape!

~ Kokyo February 24th 2016

Winds toss, high, in trees

Devestating land and dwelling.

Shadows lurk as clouds lear -

Wreackage, waste strun on landscape,

Await repair of time and toil -

What is torn apart today; is healed and cured, tomorrow.

~ Kokyo

Sea Glass

Bits of sea glass,

Polished opaque by sand and sea,

In tumultuous tide...

Picked by poet on shore,

Turned to sunlight,

Catches point of view advantage

Cast among multitude,

Some embrace luster -

Some, extract gleam!

~ Kokyo February 7th 2016

Snowflakes fall with silent thud!

Loved ones lite similarly in my heart,

Blessings gathered in years of joy & pain...

Resignation into serenity and restful ease!

~ kokyo

A few sight snow flurries,

Slant down, stinging the springtime earth.

April is becoming May.

Will relents,

Emptiness emits the ten thousand things...

And, from this promontory,

Adepts gather once more to restate the cannon...

Poems ensue, and friends gather around this world,

Awaiting the snows of aquired grace.

~Kokyo David Young

Spring Dust

Spring dust,

White over green...

Grant rest,

Blessings for the dear ones!

(That's a wide scope)

Music & poems,

And rest, oh, rest,

For the journey has been arduous and long;

May we linger moored in port,

Until decommissioned and scrapped..

Our absence registered in incense smoke, curling...

~ Kokyo

Stone

Petrified, this old and rickety,

Arm chair Buddhist, rests in a painful Nirvana,

Content to accept what arises!

~Kokyo

Sunshine

☐Sunshine,

Porch sitting sunshine;

Longtime absent, skinny dipping sunshine;

Sheep may safely graze sunshine -

Where you been half my life sunshine...

Sunshine, you come out and rock my world Sunshine -

Sunshine for my friends whose sunshine is obscured.

Sunshine who enters our world profoundly,

After interminable delay...

Grow my plants, paint my world, heal my wounds...

Give me grace to live another day...

~ Kokyo

Released,

You are free together now -

No constraints!

The sun of a warm spring day,

Melts the heavy encroaching snow of winter away...

Its rays piercing in to my psyche,

Awakening a long forgotten young boy -

The worth of winter!

~ Kokyo

Sitting, remembering youth,

In the Spring sunshine -

I tell myself the winds,

Are not as cold as Hell!

~ Kokyo

Sitting in a late spring

tinkling bells in the back garden _

a joyful ease...

~ Kokyo

Rejoicing in rest of tired body,

Celebrating an end to struggle -

The Summer's fierce heat,

Gave way to Autumn's joyful ease...

Now in Winter's evening,

Happy to embrace the approaching, silent night!

~ Kokyo

Variation on a Pop Song

In my garden,

There is serenity and grace;

The world does not impinge,

And imagination reigns as real.

~ kokyo

As I Live my Life for You
(for Ruby & Emily, with extension)

I give you all my strength,

Unstintingly,

As I live my life for you.

I devise skillful means

To alleviate your pain;

As I live my life for you.

I revive after exhausting

My reserves;

As I live my life for you.

It is my pleasure

To do all for you;

As I live my life for you.

When I have done,

And my life is spent –

I'll lay down my life for you.   ~ Kokyo

Awakened nature,

Eternal, not eternal -

Joy forever!

~ Kokyo

David, Mine Your Words

This heart is a perfect resource,

A gold mine for smelting -

A fund of diamonds, ready cut...

You have to know how to dig,

To refine; just when and how to turn to the light...

Polishing your silver,

Having cast it;

Give it a steel ring -

An alloy for tomorrow's parlance...

Strength to last the deluge!

~ Kokyo

In this dusty, wind-swept world,

Much sorrow, suffering; pain and loss...

Accept and be blessed!

~ Kokyo

For James Fraser

Tears have fallen down my cheeks,

All this day of your death...

The true man of no rank,

Will no longer come and go,

Through your sense gates.

~ Kokyo

Going Home

I said,"good-bye" to my garden,
It will be green where I'm going -
Breezes and warm buffeting winds will blow...

My family and friends will gather;
Pain will perish; joy persisting!

But, I'll bide here a while, resting, happy -
Sure of my eventual home...

Gassho

~ Kokyo

I will Give you Poems

I will give you poems in season -

Be quick to catch the lines -

I counsel and deliver,

At sunset there are threads of whisperings,

At sunrise, a motion to dismiss,

Adjourn till dusk of a nearer night,

In your garden I lurk,

Capture the glimmers lying in wait.

Shed the shredded hurt and grasping -

"Empty yourself, that you might be filled."

~ Kokyo

Even a tattered twisted branch -

If it can get the sap up from its roots,

Can bud into beauty again!

~ Kokyo

Tea with my Niece, Alix

"The beach has changed", you said;

"All is impermanent.", Buddha said -

It is enough,

That the sound of waves,

Remains the same!

~ Uncle David

Birthday Gift for my Niece, Lee

If I should uncork one of my vintage poems,
Of an evening, allowing it to breathe...
Having aged, they yield a richer bouquet,
A more mellow flavour...
Having a fine body,
It gives itself up to a refined palette –
With lingering layers that go deep.
And, if,
An intoxicated fool is heard, in peels of laughter,
To giggle and guffaw in company –
Just realize he is remembering an ancient moment,
In the Vineyard...
And if he should decant a bottle for you,
At some pertinent moment of your life...
Count yourself among his friends!

~ Kokyo Oct. 18th 2016

For my Sensei,

Tesshin-san James Smith
                &
Hojo-san Taiun Michael Elliston, Roshi

Parched

Parched, the weary earth,
Foliage yellowing in mid-summer;
Drought threatens as sultriness climbs -
Family gathers on the fatherland,
Seeking coolness of the harbour's gusty draft;
Sky scorches all below,

Animals scurring into burrows.
May the weather soon break,
Quenching all the blistered, broken terrene.

~ Kokyo

Pleasant hour of cooling,
After hot, humid afternoon-
This music in the prevening.

~ Kokyo

Haggard heartache
At sight of loved-ones' natures -
Dislodged by brutal, shuddering awakening...

~ Kokyo

Vile lawn-mower,
Obliterating , "Nights in the Gardens of Spain",
Muffled in this Garden in Pictou:

De Falla assaulted -
Felicitious interruptus.

~ Kokyo

Sadly, you have gone,
Leaving us with only our lonely rhododendron,

~ Kokyo

Moving Along

I've sat here till sunset,
Time I was moving along.

My heart goes hiding deep,
I'm going to change my song.

One more day,
Perhaps another night.
I don't plan to continue,
To put up another fight.

I go where none can find me,
Sending letters from the far side of the sun.
If you look for my old form and substance,
You'll not find me where you'd expect I'd be.

Love goes into the forest black,
In the night I am gone,
No traces, no tracks,
Don't look for me - I'll not be back.

~ Kokyo

The Priest Admonishes the World

I've watched your hearts turn putrid,
Petrified into hatred;
I can stay and watch no longer.
I'll not come out to meet you on the commons;
I will no longer keep the vigil of return,

Not being able to reciprocate as before;
If you do not turn your hearts
I no longer know you,
Step away from my sheltering door.

~ Kokyo

Harvest Moonlight

Warm summer morning air;
Dispelled, previous evening's cloudy gloom -
Breezes slip thru trembling leaves,
Beegie Adair hangs on the air;
Rumbling traffic entering town,
Starlings flock in flight, zizaging course,
As they do...

In childhood, I remember,
Standing in a copse, by a sea-bank,
My puny form looking up through tall spires,
Blue and white above pines;
There my esthetic inclinations were formed;
Then, slumbering till awakened again at 16,
By George Crawford.

As soon as resolution found,
My writing becomes limited by illness;

Then, practicing; learning; cultivating my style,
Much reading stimulating a hungry brain;
Harsh experience staggering; and then love-
Nourishing a crippled heart.

Foundation's of poetics set
15 years Garden lay fallow,
"He tells me to wait" ~ such my still-small-voice.
In middle to old age the harvest came...

Oh! Look,
Let's go dancing in the Harvest Moonlight.
These gleanings shimmering across the Harbour -
Some day we will linger on this spot,
Upon the shore.

~ Kokyo

Heed, Inverterate Hearts

Inveterate hearts, desist,
Heal to tenderness;
Soften your calcified stance,
Leading yourself and others,
To perdidition's acid sting..

Relent your intractability,
Gladly receiving the diverse;

Tolerate what you depreciate;
Less you grow stagnant in your own stench,
Rotting upon a garbage heep of Acrimony.

~ Kokyo

Somewhere There Is A Garden

Just behind your thoughts -
Trip them:
It waits to open before you,
And beyond...
Opening your rumination,
Push aside the gateless gate -
It spreads upon your heart,
Abide, dwell, invite its verdure,
Bloom, create a world-wide terrace,
Cousining the entire sentient cosmos.

~ Kokyo

Return

Music, carry me down river,
Where my face is unknown;
Deposit me on the levy,
Where I can dance in morning sun -
Washing away in tide:
Then, give my evenings
Tone of western sky,
And let me relent,
And return to settled,
Hushed, serene, eternal, source.

~ Kokyo

Beautiful

Beautiful face; beautiful heart -
My companion;
All these difficult years,
Archetypal life of suffering,
Our heart (for it is one)
Forged in Fire -
In this garden, tonight,
We pledge; we apprehend; we grasp,
The Heartland of Union,
Jumping into our heart, in concert,
"Both feet first!"*

~ Kokyo

Into Temperate Dusk

Humid - tread cool sand-bar;
Scent restoring air,
Rushing into harbour.

Remember the trope
Languish into gelid twilight -
Regret not afternoon's glare
Have a flare for evening shadows.

~ Kokyo

Gradations of Contentment

Joy, a substratal element,
Whereas, well-being's a rarer commodity;
A very plaintive cockerel.

To be satisfied evokes acceptance;
Happiness, a modest allotment,
Granted brief and singular -

So, to be joyfully serene;
Is perennially possible -
Happy, occurring only sporadically.

~ Kokyo

The Way

Butterfly, make your meandering way,
You were once a ground-restricted worm;
Consonant the way of the sun -
Butterfly or sun; wayward or direct,
Both beautify; both give grace.

We make our way; ply our trade.
The benefit is on the path;
Spending as we go; yet, amassing benediction -
To be on the roadway is to have reached home,
Arriving before we have begun.

May I see you off stage;
May we be together then.

~ Kokyo

Illumination

There is poetry in the valley,
Poetry in the hills;
The breezes blow deep or elevated...
The sunrise thundering it's music,
Along the glen; or cascading thru the ridge,

If I give you a semblance of the enthusiasm,
You can, perhaps, provide your own vivication.

~ Kokyo

Four Seasons

In Winter, garden in mordant mode -
No élan vital endowing greenery.
Spirit rummaging in stinging necrosis.
In waiting for revitalizing Spring,

Who, when she arises,
Blooms the sluggish heart-blood;
As melting mountain streams,
Cleans and refresh the decadent earth.

Comes sweltering Summer,
As nature's dance unfolds;
Love ignites in slumbering youths,
And forms Autumn's cradle.

Who's reds and golds furbish the alluvium earth -
Spent and exhausted its flurry;
Expiring in the gathering brumal Winter's
Tempestuous, unbridled, fury.

~ Kokyo

Heart's Verdure

Garden, untended,
Loses luster.

Heart left fester,
Grows mordant.

Weeding, aerating,
Adding nutrients,

Hearts awaken
Verdant, lush, nourishing...

~ kokyo

Joyous Garden

It is beyond my poetic capacity
To sing of the shelter & seclusion
Of this joyous garden;
This twittering song bird does better justice;
Enhanced by Mozart,
She sings of the serenity of this noise,
Cancelling enclosure.

My moments here, nullify also,
All harshness, sorrow & strife -
Granting me inclusion in solitude's conferal -
Nature's acceptance and bestowal,
The return of the ragged vagabond.

~Kokyo

White Ox-Cart

The yellow daffodil's flower
Is its nature;
So the poem is its face,
Face & heart, one.

The great vehicle
Is the Way;
Flower, poem, growth to fruition...

Walking; sitting -
Action, non action...
Silent Thunder.

Sitting at home;
Or on the road -
Traveling white ox-cart just the same.

~ Kokyo

Elemental

Earth, air, wind, fire;
Mountains, trees, grass, walls, pebbles;
Sun, moon, home, garden...
Night begats day; day turns to night.

In this Empty Mind -
Earth deposits -

Amber, Ruby, Emerald,
Heart's embers,
Fanned by hand of poet's wit.
Eye, ear, smell, taste, touch;
Soil sediments seeds;
Nurturing nutrients,
Sprouting shoots of Irises -
Variegated purple, yellow.
Delicate response to rain -
Exhalations of abundance.

Life, decays, becomes earth:
Provisional metaphor

Incense smoke, curling,
Is gone...

~ Kokyo   March 11, 2018

Dwelling in Emptiness

Clear timber & brush
From rugged, fertile land;
Drag with a stick to till the soil;
Sow the seed; weed & water
Till the grain grows tall.

In like manner,

Hoe & sow the heart.
Clearing out obstructive mind stuff,
Ride along on an empty heart
Hear, heed the counsel from the Source.

There is Emptiness.
It is filled.
Weed.

~ Kokyo

Wordlessly Watching

Wordlessly watching
Shadows in flight, across the ground -
Black wings drift over snow.

Sounds unheard,
Cast impressions in the heart -
Movements stir in soul.

Given that you have been with me all this time;
Seeing mute upon the day;
Gathering moments mounting mountains.

Chasing concern forward;
While I dusted clear the shabby path.
Watch now, as we fade together away...

No longer occurring our space and time.

~ Kokyo

Bloom

Falling ill in youth,
Dangling on the proverbial precipice.
Caught between Charbilysis & Scylla.
Prostrate eaten by gadflies;

My brain stung, continually ,
As though sulfuric acid dripped, dropped,
Achingly, upon my brain stem;
My mind was launched upon,
A kaleidoscopic odyssey,
A voyage of intricate madness.

Today, in old age, Ulysses is home in Ithaca -
Penelope has been liberated,
And the Adriatic is clear and azure blue.
We are home at 7 Eccles Street; we are free...

~ Kokyo

Runes

Stay with me, while the music is lovely,
Lay with me when the night turns long...

When the cold creeps, fridged, to our shoulders,
We will need each other to be strong...

When they turn our bones in distant digs,
With these runes we will convey our song...

~ Kokyo

Recollection in Old Age

The old man
Smiled compassionately
On hearing the story of the tragically conflicted
Young lovers;
He smiled in his heart,
At what had once been a sorrow,
But was today a philosophical resigned
Pity; a joy of celebration
At what once had been.

~ Kokyo

I Am The Unity You Crave For
"Within causes and conditions, time and season,
it is serene and illuminating." *

"You are not it, but in truth, it is you" *
I am The Unity you crave for -
Peace to you, and all your generations -
Your friends gather to celebrate your feast.

The Rainbow of my Covenant is above your Rakusu...
Whoever enters your gate, shall be refreshed,
My unclouded sky will penetrate to your quick,
And sadness will trouble you no longer.

They that come, will find comfort at your table,
You have offered yourself to all;
All will return to you,
Not one of your kin shall be lost!

~ kokyo
 * Soto Zen Chant, Precious Mirror Samadhi
Right Speech

I spoke untruly,

I spoke thoughtlessly in anger;
But, I have also spoken kindly,
To soothe...

I have spoken critically of you,
(seeing that which I cannot help but see).
But, I hide shame faced,
At the words which have escaped my restraint,

Have I given love in language meant to awaken.
Have I given Right Speech,
It has been given me to speak.

~ Kokyo

Sadness & Joy

There will be sadness, dear one,
And there will be grief.

But, there will be comfort,
And release.

Your heart will open
Unto an expanse so bright,
It will contain all that is,
And all that is not....

Your tears will be dried,
And you will bring Joy to many...

~ Kokyo

Lot's Lot

Residing on the edge of town;
Detractors abound,
But friends balance...

There is more awakening than of old,
But to be different is often to be scorned...

Going along heedless,
Utterly oblivious,
Well, attempting.

~ Kokyo

Kokyo

Empty of self,
Reflecting mirror:
Cloudy day,
Seemingly endless night...
Cherishing one who has cherished -

Into the ineffable...

~ Kokyo

Silence enhanced
By sound of melting snow!

~ Kokyo

Stepping off a Hundred Foot Pole

Reaching the end of my tether..
Hemmed in, no place to stand -

It is here I'll rest,

Assured, abandoning desire
For alternative lodging!

~ Kokyo

Confinement Practice

Within the limitations of your conditions -
Practice Liberation!

~ Kokyo

There is suffering;
Here, in your heart -
Enter, and be still..

~ Kokyo

SAD*

In winter,
I do shriveled raisin Zen -
My mind beclouded by darkness:

So, I sit warm, in inner light!

~ Kokyo
* Seasonal Affective Disorder
  (caused by Vitamin D Deficiency)

Exsultate Jubilate

Breeze bring home,
My love,
I sent it out some time hence

So to see what she might discover.
Until nightfall, I will send again...

Seeking after you.

Dayrise I come, searching,
Ever after till your return -

In time I find the eternal,
Now, I find you home,
Experience experiments with this springtide

~ Kokyo

Ruby

If we are blessed in life,
As I have been with you, love,
Our loneliness will end,
And all our sorrows will be healed;
Our happiness will be assured,
Even if we must swim the perilous seas,
With only perseverance as our armour.

If one is blessed,
As I have been with you, dear,
One's heart will sing soulfully,
Until the sea rushes in with the tide,
And his last expiration will be his love's name..

~ Kokyo David Young

My wife in the Window seat, drinking tea,
all who suffer in youth,
not denied future fulfillment & joy...

Suffering not permanent, sorrow not fixed

~ Kokyo

Laughing Buddha

Hotei, laughing Buddha,
Weeps...

Let his weeping bring you home.

Gathered, others return to source,
Your intrinsic nature,
Undressed, unfaced...

Given the gravity of circumstances;
We must rejoice,

Everywhere is light

In the crevices, dark,

It was ever thus -
"accept and be blessed!"

~ Kokyo

Hey Ruby!

Ruby, get up
And begin your daily dance,
With you husband;

The harpist plays her finest strain,
Replete with time's finest stain

Today, again,
We'll play in repartee:

As I rejoice in your heartfelt expressions -
"I wonder how her mother is. I miss my little girls!"

You have continued to charm my heart,
These many varied years,
Lining it with golden balm...

Enchanting my days,
In extended rapture. ..

Gassho,

~ Kokyo David

The drift

Your words drift
Into this stream

Much has been made of the round of the sun
Carrying, as it does, the daily calamity,

Perhaps, we can best respond,
With hope and challenge to aspire...

Impervious to anger
Giving rein to our best impulse

Gathering those twitching in grief, pain & sorrow,
Ushering in the setting and rising of renewable light...

~ Kokyo

Who is Waiting, Watching

Who watches and waits?
What is that presence, felt;
Who hovers; who beckons?
Beacons?

We are held in metaphorical arms;
Bosoms of blessing.
Not deviating from the precepts;
Right Action;
Right Speech and Right Thought, etc. -
We are borne upon Compassion,
The embodiments.

Never despairing; traveling ardently -
Boldly stride through the gateless gate.

~ Kokyo

Empty words
Ending talent...

Fraudulent
or legitimate
method -

Has the beautiful departed
or was Keats wrong -
Lao Tzu correct*

We'll see where it goes...

~ Kokyo
*Keats felt Truth was beauty; beauty truth
While Lao Tzu felt true words were not beautiful; beautiful words not
true

Empty,
Nothing to impart,
Joy gathered 'round my heart

Silent thunder,
Made palpable!

~ Kokyo

Absolute Beauty

Clouds clearing
Inherent Beauty shattering
Previous concepts of Real...

Clear winter moonlight,
Illumines darkened world.
All seen, infused with grace,
Beauty, before unglimpsed, now all embracing...

We cannot depart from THIS,
(Except apparently)

Tragedy of unperceived awakening!

~Kokyo

Poetic Creation

Sometimes your strength
And aspirations rise
Very high

You achieve,
Immaculate conception,

Unsummoned,
Spontaneous,
Arising out of the vacuous ether...

Satisfyingly, polished -
Entering into our lexicon,

Replenished.

~ Kokyo

A Brief History of the Poem

Your strategy, your sacrifice,
Not to impede the poem.
The way, unblazed,
Unknown, and untried...

She, empirical archetype,
Arriving soon from the East,
Enchanting, alluring,
An orchid.

All the various Bodhisattvas
All along the Northumberland strait
& Atlantic seaboard.
On stage - timing impeccable.

Now, hinterland,
Fertile, fecund -
Ground, cleared, broken,
& plowed.

Planting,
Cultivating, in time, a wheat field -
A bowl for tomorrow's children.

~ Kokyo

Impermanence
(for my granddaughter, Emily)

Change comes rarely without sorrow,
And so, your 13th birthday makes me sad -

For, as someone said, of our young children,
"Where do they go?"

But, with change comes renewal,
And here we have a newly arrived Youth,

One who is indeed familiar,
The much admired fruition,
Of your formative years,

Our little girl,
Beautiful, gracious, mature;
Intelligent, kind, and wise!

~ Kokyo Papa

The Salvatory Nature of Kwan Yin

Compassion sweeps Kwan Yin,
Hauntingly across an ocean of time,
Delivering my past;
Gathering us up unto a shaft,
Of love, lovingly lifted.

Here, in this stratosphere,
Pain can still reach;
Hell, it can destroy -
But, with next breath, Kwan Yin,

Stream of Nirvana, swoops our remnant
Into joyzone restoring layer, acquiesced.

~ Kokyo

Zazen

Zazen restores
"a place to go"*
Illness creates poetry.
Family of kind, gracious friends,
Fostering.
Sunshine settles seat of Mind...
Rest in dharmakaya.
Joy & Sorrow come to all,

~ Kokyo
* "When you have Zazen, you always have a place to go!"
        ~ Soyu Matsuoka Roshi

Haven't a lot to Say

Haven't a lot to say...
ease of body, ease of mind,
cord of restful ease,
give this practice to empty world
allow the entrance
encourage the relenting,
Entering this gateless gate.*

~ Kokyo
* Zaikei Tukodo, "Entering the Gate", ceremony initiating a Priest in
Training, Soto Zen; and by extension, figuratively.

Carthage

I am the heaviness
Which the lightness must leaven -
The tardy monk who falsified the rule...

Yet, I survived the torrent;
Living, awakened, in a calcified carcass.

I have not the usual practitioners blyth action;
I am he who waits by the shore...

Content,
To have risen from the Carthaginian ashes.

~ Kokyo

Death Watch

Death hovers,
Over the family.
The nephew watches
Through day and night -
Goodbyes have been said;
Memories recalled; bonds affirmed -
We wait under strain astounded.

~ Kokyo

Porgi Amor

Subsequent to this
Will be given
the gift...
They're going home.

Dawn
Finds us awake all night
Bury our care
Empty our burden
Return, release
I'll be there in the morning.

~ Kokyo

Op. 111

Last composed
Greatest gift,
Ludwig can I requite?

Washing done, natural
Path.
Instructive mundra
May it be.

Apparently to realize
Empty to

~ Kokyo

Parinirvana

If I had rest,
I would lay my head on Erda's breast;
Surrendering my cautions and cares,
Relaxing into the profound sunyata of return -

My woes would end;
Those I love, waiting,
Would caress me in their insubstantial arms,
And I would melt, like ghee,
Into a serene & joyful, intimate Nirvana.

~ Kokyo

4f

4f from participation?
Ticket to rich experience

Pain, suffering,
Life exists not without a dose
Inoculation against terror,
Passage to Joy

~ Kokyo

Miss-Speak

Missunderstanding
Is built on miss-speaking...
"you have to be very careful what you say!"

Or miss-hearing,
Hearing what you think is being said.

I do hope I have spoken correctly

~ Kokyo

Reticence

My sister and I
Had a restrained relationship

But, in her final years,

She would often meet me as I walked to town,
Pick me up, and we would talk on the way to the mail.

It is times, like these, of simple closeness
Which I cherish now,

Forgotten is the strain.
Remembered are her many kindnesses,
Unperceived, or misconstrued,
Before.

~ Kokyo

I love

I love
Songs sing thru me
Organs resoundingly love
Sing my songs

Growing and decaying
Sixty-nine years tomorrow

Joy
All spinal Joy
Body vibrating Joy
Emote my love

To you reader,
To you.

~ Kokyo

The Empty Mind
(an utterance of..)
(As you are It, to be lost In It, is to be)

In the eye which is my mind,I see her
(God(dess), Buddha, Alla, Dao),
Expansive, extending in all directions,
Calling with her Beauty -

Filled with awe, with wonder, with Joy,
Tasting the unpopulated serenity,
Of The Empty Mind...
The Breath of the Utterance of

~ Kokyo

Sit

Sitting mountain
Firm.

Care
Regard
Faith firm

Be
Until others
Arrive
Free

We'll see

~ Kokyo

69th Kokyo Birthday Song *
(feeling not to shabby)
* with a nod to Paul Simon

Resting more,
Leisurely writing,
Emily, Shawn, & Bella arrive.
Greetings from afar.
Ruby gave me a book on mysticism
By the Dalai Lama -
He knows how to practice "Right Speech".

I'm 65% Theravadin - 35% Mahayanist ....I subscribe to Nirvana as end state. One lifetime .
All enter Para-Nirvana upon death.

But, if you're unhappy; I am unhappy

~ Kokyo

"Die on your cushion! "*
* Taiun Michael Elliston, Roshi

Sibelius says, "give it up!"
Resting, recreate in the Void.

~ Kokyo

Fleeting Shadows

Emotions fleeting,
In this illusory dreamworld -
As well they may,
One skip from sorrow to joy,
Returning again to sadness...

How fortunate in this empty mind,
Where nothing stays for long,

One fleeting shadow following another...

~ Kokyo

Among the Awakened

When with them there is a palpable presence,
A reasurrance;
Something tangible to the heart/mind.

They can awaken by their being with..
The hushful peace of a temple;
The gentle humor of a master.

Your trembling ceases: your footsteps sure...
They will answer before you ask...

Only just listen to the "transmission by mind"
Before you can find your mind,
It is pacified...

~ Kokyo

Joy Comes

Joy comes not
When we overcome -
Joy overcomes!

Priming Joy's pump,
With forced Joy -
Well wells up
Joyfully!

Kokyo

Family Way

Flair up; quickly mollified. ..
Traditions of character handed down -
Family understanding...
In-laws chosen to suit, eventually,
Sympatico.

The Family Way.

~ Kokyo

I and Thou

There has always been a you & me -
Two trees have grown together.

There has always been an Ich Und Du,
These trees withstood all weather.

Trees that stand; will fall in time...
But, you & me, forever...

~ Kokyo David Young

Safe in the Soup *

Energy come from afar,
Safe in the Soup.
Enter my cave,
But keep your distance.
I remember from before,
We will be together after.

Experience makes us wary;
Practice renders us open.
If I give today,
I collect tomorrow.
Music makes me mild -
Your words drive me crazy.

Going & coming -
If I remain, I am gone!

~ Kokyo
* Buddha likened Nirvana to a soup in which we are all individual spices.

Dokusan

If "poetry is posey",

Then, poetry is posturing...
My father did an action, a posture,
(Laying down his life for me),
So that I might do an action,
(Taking up my life),
Life as action, making my expressions,
Posturing,
But, (Dharma, no Dharma),
Silence, the true expression, is transmission:

~ Kokyo

Gorgonzola

Ate the Gorgon last night,
Vivid dreams followed...

Father's home, we siblings as ghosts...
Jon tried to break my reserve,
Leaves kitchen, (after Dad's Death)
I break into sobs, catharsis.
Unity...

Fragment of a Reconstruction

~ Kokyo

How Vast the Robe of Liberation

Tenacious difficulty?
Resolve into Nothingness -
Empty circumstances,
Gathered turmoil,
Dissolving into glee...

Assembled on this shore,
Preparing departure -
Embark upon quest,
Sailing sea of conditions,
Detached from previously
Presumed entanglement...

Liberated, freed,
Flavours in the sauce -
Spread upon the loaf!

~ Kokyo

Milkman's Route

Seems sometimes
A milkman's route's
The clearest path we have -

We each must make our game plan
Adopt, then fashion, the rules of play.

Acting out each moment
Caution with abandon -
Passing being, eternal now*..

Music of the movement,
Chorus of continuum.

~ Kokyo
* eternal now, Paul Tillich's phrase

Rorschach

Each poem a screen,
Project your own poem (PYOP)

~ Kokyo

Forever By The River Skipping Stones

We are waiting by the river to cross together
(We went wrong by clinging to the right)
In the twilight we cross over to the other shore.

With assaults to our Precepts we've grown obese.
Like our ecosystems, we are polluted.
Our ignorance appalls; dejected without hope.

By water, waiting -
Single or severally shall you come,
Watching, catching sight of morning star,
We are forever by the river skipping stones...

~ Kokyo

Word Salads

"Since I left confusion behind 30 years ago I have never lacked for salt or
sauce to eat"
            ~ Ma-tsu, Zen Master

Word salads,

Some profound,
Some prosaic.

Pepper with flavours,
Garnished with alliterations

Gathering garden vegetables,
Protein from the poultry.

Poems, simply menus,
Weed, harvested, preparing:

Chef-boyardee, est tu!

~ Kokyo

Grey Day

There is something about a grey day -
Pleasant, taking it for what it is,
Contemplative:
Teaching, in itself, the joy of suchness!

~ Kokyo

Time of Trouble

Your heads were haunted,
By the harm of the wind darkening night,
When, running the rain swept street,
The Trouble trampled, tarnishing hearts -
Turned sickly and jaundiced,
By cruel, harsh, experience.

In compassionate sympathy,
I cried, throughout the ages with you,
When no balm would heal your Parsifal
Wounds.

How will it end?
When, ever, will you see again the sun -
When will the hurt, the sting,
Be lifted from your storied faces,
And your crystal laughter, gurgle up, restoredly again?

~ Kokyo

So Much Sorrow and Suffering

So much sorrow and suffering,

Can Buddhist Practice relieve,
The most atrocious suffering?

In my own experience,
With mental illness,
I answer yes.

In suffering, such as brutality,
Slavery, torture, war, third world conditions?

I hope so;
But that, for me, is an unknown...

~ Kokyo

Absolute Beauty

Opening the mind to Absolute Beauty -
Abiding there...

~ Kokyo

Loved Ones Past

Loved ones past, yet present:

Fraser & Cassie (my Dad, deeply tragic & Mum by grief, no words!);
Hill & Pearl (beloved Aunts);
Sam & Lucy (Loved, Father-in-& law & Mother-in-law);
Bruce, Margie & Gwen (Brother & Sister in-laws & Niece by marriage, children of tragedy);
Debbie & Tanya (Niece by marriage & Great Niece by marriage, gone too soon, sadly missed);
Shannon & James (harshly ended)
Gerry, Kath & Sandy (loved, Brother, Sister & Brother-in-Law);
Clarence & Clarence (Uncle & Brother-in-law, my uncle's name sake {curiously});
Robert (Loved Cousin)
Ethel, Jim, Belle (my mother's siblings, dear ones);
Henry, (dear Henry, Brother-in-law);
Donnie & Ella (cherished cousins);
Jeannie (cherished Cousin);

Surround and protect us, as they do:
Host of Heaven, leading, we aspire to thee.

~ kokyo

Peace of Completion

Samadhi Samadhi Samadhi

Peace passing comprehension...

Completion;
All marbles in a row...

Relaxing into evening,
Ground; structures; capping phrases -

Murmurs of contentment;
Contentions surpassed,
Evening colors merge;

Diamond Cutter creation;
Golden Dragon sleeping...

~ Kokyo

Wormholes Winding into the Mystic Woods

All our, sights, sounds, tastes, touch, minding
All occurences, happenings, stimuli -
Wormholes into the Mystic wood...

Grasp, grapple, wrest into insight,
Gather gapeings, breaking into Beauty!

Out unto the plain, nourish on grains,
Remain, be bread baskets to the world.

~ Kokyo

Ground Zero

Foolish frenzy
Vacant mind,

Yielding vast concerns -
Given time,
Wasted worlds reworld,
Reword rewards accrue

I was not meant to fail yet,
Safe, yet perilous close to doom.

The woe man's land
Wo man acquire

She will the will aspire than expire...
Let us not cry over spilt breastfeeding

We enquire into teleological evenings!

~ Kokyo

Release the Dove

Release the dove,
Evolve the b(t)rain,
Trace the travellers on the track.
The Godhead increases by expressions,
She increases by experience,
Affluent in fluency.
Utterances timely instep.

~ Kokyo

Sarnath

Site of first sutra
Opening unto morning star
Transmission of mind
Revolving the wheel.

Compassion accomplished
Beauty beheld
Awe aspired

Inspiring cast forth
Meaning of the coming from the west

Till today expanded,
Expanding still

Going to becoming
Being to nothingness,
Ten thousand things (e)merge...
Dharma no Dharma

Transmission of mind by my illness
and the Southern school -
Give us this day,
Received as it is:
Being-in-itself

~ Kokyo

444

Mary Rose, the other day, spoke of meaning
Of 444, as "all watched over by Angels of loving grace."

As I reflected tonight, after writing, "Loved Ones",
The time was 4:44

~ Kokyo

Noted Poem

Zazen balm
Mercy to the future
Debating on the feasibility of Life vs. Death.
Winter is a struggle -
Kwannon weeps profusely
Worldwide release...
Well, we don't know, do we
One of fair mind, sensing a lost-leader,
Desperate for control of congressional
Hearings, the crux.

~ Kokyo

Still-Small Voice

Closer,
Approaching,
Your father,

Your granddaughter -

Walk to Me,
Measure your moments.
Aspire to create,
Gathering the impressions

I counsel you,
Attend.
It will be alright,
No fear,
Relax, recieve, review,

Rest, relinquish, return...

~ Kokyo

Side by Side

Not two,
Do Not divide,
Decide

This gift,
You'll harness,
For relenting

Keep time:

Epitome
The Vastness

Expanding,
Containing All
Not two...

~ Kokyo

The Warp & The Weave of the Kokyo Tapestry

Follow along to the song of Kokyo,
Enter his chamber, view his tapestry.

Begin with the sonorous lapping of harbour waves
Then follow the tortuous wrack of the pain,
As he vomits his brains, till not but illness remains.

Then watch as he climbs into the marriage car;
Repacking his mind in the shape of a bard.

Now, see him recover his health in the poem,
As Zazen endeavor will lead him to home.

All within chambers unfolding his tale,
Not leaving his property, it is said, for generations.

Glide with him as he slides to the shore;

Awaiting you briefly; you'll see him no more.

~ Kokyo

Variegated Lilacs scent my eyes,

Mozart piano concerto tastes on my ears...

Cooling evening breezes as sinking sun sets

An hour reading in my garden,

After this busy, strenuous day;

Warmth finally arrived –

And my heart settles, in my greening haven

~ Kokyo

Remembrances of Pearl Gertrude Young,

Missionary to China

My earliest memories of my Aunt Pearl were vague and barely formed. She returned on furlough from China only every five years, so that I would have met her only a few times before becoming an adult.

I remember her telling us the story of she and her co-worker being detained in a town held by the Communists Chinese, when the Communists were plotting to bury them alive, two freshly dug graves awaiting them. The minister who was being held with them, who had knowledge that the Nationalist Army was set to retake the town; would answer his interrogators questions with lengthy sermons, in order to stall for time. Soon the guns were heard outside the town, signalling that the Nationalist had arrived...meanwhile, the Christian group in Germany affiliated with Pearl, began earnestly praying for them, they knew not why were praying; only that they felt it necessary.

My next memory, is of Pearl, visiting my family home when I was in my late teens.

As she was leaving, she turned to me and said, "God calls to you, David!"...today, as I recall this, it feels like a lifeline; while at the time, my reception was mixed – my dear Aunt must have been saddened by my look of astonishment.

The seeds were planted then; or at least, watered, as I recall my habitual fervent prayers as a child. These must have stemmed in a large part from Pearl. It was not part of our discussions as children.

On that same furlough, as I recall , or perhaps five years later, I remember Pearl visiting me in my sick bed at home. Pearl is one of those rare persons gifted with a presence; and I felt her "healing presence" then, feeling the love communicated in her simple words. "Yes!" she said, and she said so much with that single word. I heard her say this, so lovingly, to my father a few months before his untimely, tragic death.

By the time Pearl (I called her simply, Pearl – my wonderful Aunt Hil's "decree" {Pearl's expression } as she did not wish to be called Aunt Hil, I presume) and I meet again, I am newly and happily married, Hil brings Pearl to meet us, she exclaiming, "praise the Lord!" when she sees me beaming with Joy!

My next memory, is probably on her next five year furlough, when we had a chance to talk, just the two of us, and compare thoughts on Religion. ..it must have been this time that she told me, since I am Buddhist, "There is nothing in Buddhist philosophy which I cannot accept, David. Buddhist philosophy is beautiful. I could become a Buddhist, except that, as a Christian, I cannot bow to a statue."

I recall a visit from Pearl in our home on Alfred St. (Ruby, my wife's, family home, before we built in the backyard). At this time, I recall some snatches of conversation:

"But, I do try, Pearl!"

"What do you try?"

"Effort,"

"Well, there is no effort in this"

"Well, do you talk to God?"

"Yes, I do."

"What does he tell you?"

"He tells me to wait, "

"That's fine then!"

After "laying hands" on me, upon leaving that day, she , turning at the doorway, said,

"Do you mind me doing that? "

"No, I don't mind."

This must have satisfied her, she knew it "took." (her prayer for me was that God would make me teachable – a prayer which has been answered.)

In sum, my Aunt Pearl communicated with her person as much as with her words...it was a transmission of mind, like the Zen Buddhist speak of. And I believe she was fully participant in the Zen Buddhist Enlightenment.

With these few, brief, encounters, she altered and influenced me very profoundly. I hope I have made her live, in some way, for you!

Kokyo David Edgar Young June 6
2017

Following the way,

Summer and winter,

Spring and fall -

All my life I have been devoted to study...

Now, happy in my garden in old age,

Joyful and serene, I sing my easy songs!

~ Kokyo

A Rippling

Weight of body ache –

Decays precursor;

Wagner bringing evening –

Dampens bones into inflammation.

Acceptance making ageing easy;

Cast upon the shore,

Waiting, with forbearance,

For the longer boats across the pond.

Attracted to the slender reeds and lilies,

Strewn, as they are, along the muddy bank;

No longer, as Narcissus, gazing...

Empty of image; nothing special –

A shiver of wind upon the pool.

~ Kokyo

Enrichment

We are meant, by our living,
To enrich our heart/minds;
Gathering fodder.

If you suffer,
Suffer to enrich.

If ill; broken; lost; alienated -
Separated; cast out; castigated -
Enrich.

Accepting Karma;
Mitigates,
Following the watercourse way*

~ Kokyo
* nod to Alan Watts

Form is Emptiness *

A rest, so deep,
That, love, that, salient death,
Is implied;

And the air, my body,
My heart, are one insubstantial unity.

The Joy, the exalted exuberance,
Dissolving my being,
Into an expiration of refreshed dispersal...

~ Kokyo
* title from the Heart Sutra

As Tyranny Threatens

Feeling warm,

In this welcome sunlight,

Like melting butter...

The Orange Grunt, in office,

Not intruding here...

It is the unseen clouds which threaten

Most calamitous in the South...

~ Kokyo

Palpable Stillness

I sit,

In the darkest hour before dawn;

Stillness palpable.

The old Tao poems, still applicable...

The ancient sentiments, yet apply.

Returned to the source,

The ten thousand things resound!

~ Kokyo

Morning Shower

I am thankful for my religion, which has me sitting zazen at sunrise each morning, greeted by the same robin, as he awakes and sings of his morning chill in the cold spring air after the morning shower. In this life, we also have showers and storms. But, like the flowers, the rain nurtures us and the storms teach us resilience. The sun returns - and, because we have drunk the rain of suffering, we can now flower.

~ Kokyo

Rain,

Flowers drink,

As I drink in Ruby's quiet company...

Rhododendron beauty -

Ineluctable mystery of our union.

~ Kokyo

Great Heart

Great Heart,

Gentle, kind, prompting –

My prime mover –

You have lead me scorching,

Throughout the furnace.

Along the precipitous crags we crept.

You nourished me in the desert;

My silent voice!

Opening unto me,

You lead me to table, I dined.

After my tortuous labours in the fields –

You have lead me, these years to pasture...

In the sunlight, I have prospered.

Offering my voice to you,

I sang –

Grant, now, that my songs be heard,

Echoing over the valley,

Rumbling on the plain,

Reaching those who suffer now,

Encased in the fiery furnace.

Kokyo June 2017

Closures

I see the closing of the day;
The times have eroded the bedrock -
Our memory of how we arrived, departs,
As the vigorous tides withdraw.

My mind numbs on the residue of circumstance,
While my parched memories leave

Not closing the final door.

With you, my dear, growing feeble;
I remain, more and more,
Your loving, tender companion.
For you, I will watch the times depart,
Sheltering you from the swelter and the crime.

~ Kokyo

Not built for strenuous practice,

This is a slow horse,

Zazen, gentle, restful...

No place to be,

No axe to grind.

~ kokyo

Memories

Girl dancing,

Legs akimbo –

Music swings;

Girl pounces –

Tumbling embrace...

Nestling in dark evening wood

With love that is understanding,

They part

Remaining with each other as they go...

~ Kokyo

Open Letter to My Granddaughter

Precious Emily,

I want to tell you of how I coped in life; of how I found my way. And maybe then it will help you along your way in life.

I have found it useful, as my dear Aunt Pearl taught me, to always seek God's word in life. By this I mean, to continuously listen for you "still small voice" as it silently speaks to you in your heart. This is spoken of, as Moses is on Mount Sinai in the desert, in Exodus, the book of the old testament.

This is the "wonderful councillor", of Handel's Messiah, the musical oratorio.

I have sought this silent voice at many times in my life, and it gave me guidance and peace and joy.

When you struggle, you will find it is often easier, and the best policy, to accept your nature and circumstances, when they prove resistant to change. And it is easier to change the manner in which you react to events and persons, than to change the events and persons themselves; and, by changing yourself, you can often times change these others.

Go easy on yourself; Be your own best friend; and don't beat up on yourself. Honour yourself, you are a child of God; and a blessing to your family. When you despair, look to the beauty of your own heart, where you will find God, your comforter, not a harsh and cruel judge.

Never give up; what is bleak today, will look better tomorrow, and no sorrow need last forever.

I love you, always have and always will. Nothing can change that. Believe in that. I will always be with you in your heart, you have been the Joy of mine!

~ Papa

I have had a wonderful life. At one point, I thought I had lost everything; only to realize later, I always had it all...what I had thought was a dearth of experience, was a cornucopia of rich and prismatic experience.

In retrospect, my life has been filled with so many wonderful people manifesting as family, friends, & lovers...all giving me such texture, adding a fine grain to my full life.

Value your days, harsh & happy...the light of memory will cast them in gold!

~ Kokyo

An Old Married Couple

An old married couple,
Trundled thunderingly down the years;
At first, irascible, with ungoverned natures;
They learned, in time the practice of patience.

Devotedly they clung, lovingly, to each other;
As wolves of wild calamity
Clambered severally through their door -
All the vagaries of life visiting variously.

Vicariously they bore others sorrows;
As disability claimed her wage.
Today they reach for each other in the night,
She seeking his hand as along times lane
They stroll...

~ Kokyo
Summer Rain

I wish to be with you,
As the refreshment of a summer's rain,
Washing, clear, your troubled world ...

Undressing your readied expressions,
Gracing your hearts,
As a cooling brook, singing its gurgling Joy,
Along its winding bed,
swerving with gathered delight,
before emptying, at last,
Into its full and waiting harbour...

~ Kokyo

The Death Squeeze

Heart thickens; body tightens...
Breath shortens; activity lessens.

Constriction of flesh, presages,
Liberation of heart/mind into

Openness......

~ Kokyo

I Have Borne My Life With Courage

I have borne
My burden courageously,
All my life;
Hurricane of hardship,
Happiness hampered;
I did bare the pain my whole life long.
Stinging shafts of pain,
Mercurial management of my illness -
The reigns difficult to grasp.
Faith, Prayer, Buddhist Practice;
Wife, Family, Friends, Drs. & Nurses -
Helping me in my struggling.
Haggard till the end,
Always mitigated by Joy!

~ Kokyo

One of the "Thousand Natural Shocks"

Your news broke me.
Your years, our years,
Have been horrid hard -

Yet I remember when joys were easy, and innocent;

Caging horse rides and tripping over blades of grass;
Swimming, dining, and chanting over the promontory....

The future of "us", the four of us, is uncertain,
Although the will remains...
Frozen in prayer/zazen,
I cast a wish out the unto strait, into the future...

~ Kokyo

My Years

My years,
Folk songs and pain...
Ryokan and sandy beach...
Ruby and poetry -

Years of struggle,
Years of Joy like bluest sky.
Madness, turmoil,
The Death of those we loved -

Now, in this garden,
Sorrow still can strike -
But it is all sweetly mitigated,
By you, princess of my heart,
Glad Sun of my world.

~ Kokyo

Full moon & morning star!
Slowly birds awaken...
So too Sakyamuni Buddha,
Twenty-five hundred years ago -

Woke up!

~ Kokyo

Rain, tap
    Tap
        Taping,
Indenting leaves...

Breeze sings through swaying branches
Here and there...

Background of car tires
On wet pavement...

Basal rumble of occasional
Passing motors....

NATURE'S WIND AND RAIN CONCERTO

~ Kokyo

Powerless

I have often felt powerless,

To effect the changes

Altering situations, people, circumstances,

In a manner for lasting good...

I often wished the words to edify;

To dissuade; to prompt to rectify.

But I have found myself caring,

But impotent –

Unable to plead, to make clear the case –

To modify, to mollify.

But, continually,

I have attempted to remain steadfast and loyal,

Against all persuasion contrary....

Despite repeated offense.

Sometimes all we can,

(And this is the hardest),

Is watch them suffer,

Beyond our reach and control

~ Kokyo

Tesshin says,

"You were probably a Zen Practitioner

before you were 'you'; and you will probably be a Zen Practitioner

long after you cease to be 'you'. "

Suffering is universal and continuing...

Illness our existential state.

It links us all,

Essential to our humanity...

To "suffer with" is admirable,

A way of liberation.

We are all in the same bitter soup...

Practice, the sweetening spice!

~ Kokyo

I Will Tell It....

I well tell it...

He had the moon –

His father bought it for him.

He had his mind –

A promise of sunrise...

Sorry, nightfall! !!

Mind gone; family gone; career gone...

His mind, a wreckage of mega-storm...

Sting of gadfly; menacing anxiety –

Loss of all seemingly.

But he could connect to joy,

Then he found a Bodhisattva.

Began to rebuild;

They clung to the cliff, inching along...

Years pass, mind, new family,

All restored....

Now, a cottage on the promontory,

Beacon

~ Kokyo

Sitting endlessly,

Under winter moonlight –

Car leaving town,

Seen brief under shimmering street lamp –

Gone!

~ Kokyo

Empty mind,

fall winds rush through leaves -

Sweeping clean the obstructions of the fleeting year.

~ Kokyo

What, where, we go to,
So profound,
Words cannot twist out its shape;
A Peace, a Joy, so resoundingly intimate
An eternal inconceivable rest...

How it will transpire in Emptiness,
Ineffable...

~ Kokyo

Anti-Drab

Although I age
In the same manner as others,

My heart has a joyful swagger!

Kokyo

Kwan Yin Barbara

(Written for my dear friend, Barb Poirier,

for her birthday, Nov 7, 2016)

Mighty warrior, Zimbabwe

Bodhisattva of Compassion,

Seated on the bank of the River of Suffering,

Hearing the cries of the wretched ...

She takes action;

(Organizing clothing air drops,

Fundraising) with her skilful means,

Bringing mercy everywhere...

Like Vimalakirti, she becomes ill,

As a teaching method,

Taking on other's sorrow...

Are they her tears or theirs?

A Phoenix, who repeatedly crashes and burns,

She ever rises from her ashes...

Long may she rise – so,

Raise a glass of Vino, to our loving, Mother Courage!

~ Kokyo David Edgar Young

Kwan Yin

Sits on the Bank of the River of the World's Tears –

Her hem, soaked by the river,

Or her own tears?

She hears the cries of the suffering,

Responds, in us, her Bodhisattvas...

She mitigates, assuages,

In us, her Bodhisattvas. ..

Empty heart, free of obstructions,

Allowing Kwan Yin access –

Compassion heals sorrow...

Strength of mountain

Sitting sure and light –

What arises, easily departs.

~ Kokyo

Fixative

For those sad,

Grief stricken;

Of habitual aching mind –

Whose relationships

Are not easily amenable to alteration:

With an awakened heart,

Supplying your own balm;

Your sought for fixative –

Your own compassionate mind

Delivers you to comfort -

Healing trampled, jaded hearts.

~ Kokyo

Eschatology

Do your assigned tasks

With deliberation and diligence

Gather the remnants

For the frantic feast

Return the keys,

At the appointed hour, for,

The fabric was imagination

The form, my dears,

Was dreams and dust

~ Kokyo

Breaking winter's silence,

Suddenly, yellow warbler -

Says it all!

~ Kokyo

Garden Again

Acquiesced to limitations of age and illness,

Following the course of easy nature –

Sitting in my garden,

Warm breezes from the south,

Send all the news I need!

~ Kokyo

Snowflakes falling from eyes,

Into the brook of my heart -

Melting!

Kokyo

Stepping of the raft of thought,

Absorbed in the flowing river....

Drifting home to the sea....

Resonates with resident of the heart.

~ Kokyo

Vacancy -

Tip-toeing across the sky...

Resting on the crescent moon!

~ nobodaddy

Emptiness Bread

Leavening agent (suffering)

Sifting the flour (experience),

Kneading Nothing....

Rising in the zazen oven –

A loaf's loaf!

~ Kokyo

Even practicing alone,

good for nothing & nobody –

We are still Bodhisattvas,

Using skillful means

~ Kokyo

Until You Are Here With Me

If my theme were the world's sorrow;

Would it not be my purpose to make it mine?

At least to minimize it with my own compassion;

My action not being your action...

If we are all in the same concoction,

Will not my sorrow commensurate with yours -

And can I leave until you are here with me...

Joyfully not alone!

~ Kokyo

Snowy sleet slopes in evening street lights,
Like my last expiration -
Lost in the night...

~ Kokyo

As we walked out in morning's meadow,

We played over kisses and caresses...

Unaware that noon hour soon would

Scorch our love in sorrow...

And afternoon thunder render us

Startled into gloom's heavy skies...

Now, here,

At sunset we are vacant,

Silently, solemnly, slipping into night...

~ Kokyo

In my practice,

The moonlight enters deeply into the pool of my heart;

I, walking, skillfully, along it's golden beams,

Nursing my heart wounds with its healing light.

Now, I hang it upwards in the evening sky,

Tilting its rays downward, into your, waiting,

Shimmering pool.

~Kokyo

For close unto 70 years,

This dew drop reflected the moon...

Soon to be eclipsed!

~ Kokyo

Hope in Time of Terror

We quiver and we quake;

We tremble with downcast eyes -

Not seeing where we are going,

Not aware where we are.

We have struggled down the years

Making monumental strides;

Yet, hindered we are by ignorance,

And ungoverned by what is wise.

Now, we hasten to journey's end...

We trust, we hope, we despair.

And if the morning breaks

Finding us on the farther shore...

Surely we no longer suffer,

And we will ride on one continuum of Joy.

~ Kokyo

Sky in the head...

We are here & beyond...

There & gone...

Where we are is our home,

We have arrived before we've begun!

~ Kokyo

It is early Spring,

It is not yet Summer.

If it were Summer,

The shrubs would be green and flowering;

Birds would flit from bush to bush,

And the breezes would blow warmly.

But it is not yet Summer –

It is early Spring.

~ Kokyo

Structure

Night scheme,

Dark skies –

Quiet leaves tumbling,

Winds abating...

I am here with all gone ahead,

All collect and will collect,

In this single heart,

Containing all –

All in all.

One emotion manifests as all,

At any given time...

Joy serves as realized compassion.

Busily dusting my minds floor,

I gape and grin...

Happy with the innate structure it all!

~ Kokyo

Inchoate Strife

(Sensei Taiun would say 'attrition')
By which the world is structured,
Innately;
Instructs, and forms Awakening Beings
From its suffering.

Take the example of Jesus,
Or Buddha –
Their creed created by friction
Between what is and what is wished...

Give up wishing,
What is becomes the wish!
~ Kokyo

Intrinsic Nature

(or Original Nature,

according to Hui-neng, the Sixth Patriarch)

The Kingdom of Heaven Within , of Christ.

(an ox and a donkey ride in)

Your 'original face,

The face you had before your mother

And father were born –'

Where is it right now?

This nature which undressed nature,

The face of the Void!

~ Kokyo

Nadia's Forest

Nady, my friend,

Treads softly on the mossy forest,

Scattered with ferns.

Sunlight streams dappled through

Evergreen canopy.

Birds flit and sing, while,

Occasionally wildlife traces are found...

In my summers in childhood,

I knew forest wonders,

The sheltering peace and breath of the trees

Nurtured and forming my soul...

May dear Nadia, long enjoy,

Her wondrous woodland enchantment!

~ Kokyo

Lost Restored

The night your car, my father, crushed your chest,
My world shattering as well;
Mother, you dying, of grief, some time later -

Kicked out of Eden,
Ill, and frozen in the rainy night,
Lead, only by the full moon's light,
To your lonely door.

Captured by you, Kwan Yin,
With your alluring heart...

In time we rebuilt our several worlds,
Until we sit, now, in a meadow, grassy
Empty of a lifetime of the world's care,
At ease, our family & friends, restored.

~ Kokyo

Michael

A bright, clear summer morning,

I am nine or ten,

My brother and I

Row the blue, calm harbour,

Across to Pictou Light...

We sing Michael Row the Boat Ashore.

Not one hundred yards away,

Our parents hear our strong, innocent,

Harmonious voices over pure, quiet water...

Just now, in dream,

"Shining brighter onto the perfect day,"

In two-part harmony, I sing

The same, clear and bright song,

To my parents, listening,

Across the hall...the Other Shore!

I come...to light!

~ Kokyo

Conclave of Form and Emptiness

Do you,
I wonder, dear one,
See cloud-clearing blue;
Hush of bird-twittering dawning,
When aspirations rise...
For, to aspire is to arrive,
In that Conclave of Form & Emptiness.

~ Kokyo

We grow old,
Our minds fading -
Dandelion gossamer!

~ Kokyo

Incense

an old friend departs,
leaving the smoke of our friendship
curling 'round my heart.

~ Kokyo

Winds of torment
Chased me around -
Standing my ground, enduring,
Defeated them...

~ Kokyo

Letter to My Aunt Pearl (deceased)

What direction....waiting, all comes
You have done, david...travel lite-hearted

And in the end...we do not know, but He does
Too easy...i'm just me

And music...'tis your delight
My poetry...illustrative

My loved ones...all enfolded
Is he satisfied...most assuredly

Goodnight...Goodnight

~ Kokyo

(Tesshin said,"40% of Buddhist Practice is
working with materials.")

Words as material -
The matter of the Way,
Does it Matter? - -
It sure does!

~ Kokyo

Stealth Full breezes
Hush through Forsythia -

Silent Thunder!

~ Kokyo

Those we love and have loved -
Memories soft hued, nourishing
A cornucopia of love -

You rest with me, enduring...

~ Kokyo

They told us you are leaving;
No Milo, no Meghan, no Marie -
The neighbourhood is losing too many friends!

Depleted.

~ Kokyo

Sitting up late night
With illness:
No concern; fulfilled,
Accomplished...
Disappearing into night -
It's alright!

~ Kokyo

Ruby I live in your heart, always,
I do not squirm

~ Dave

Dwelling in my garden,
Amid the noise and boisterousness
Of this sorry age -
May the scent of Beauty Bush pervade!

~ Kokyo

Unto Forsythia,
Songbird alites,
Thrilling her joyous peal -

Noise nullifying song!

~ Kokyo

Writing Poems

A word is out -
"a stone, a leaf, an unfound door."*
Door opens, emerging from emptiness
Poems ensue:

~ Kokyo
* Thomas Wolfe,
Assimilating
Ignorance

Ignorance is imploding:
A little here, a little there -
Bits of ignorance everywhere

~ Kokyo

Heart as Garden

Leaf cups,

Music pleasing to the eye,
Sprays of flowering bushes,
Scented on draughts of Summer air;
Shitsu exploring garden;
Entering this heart,
Your perfume lingers;
All who come are welcome;
Departing, not pursued.

~ Kokyo

Aesthetics

Ruddy brown,
Earth-mind,
Garden heart-bed,
Kept weeded, tended,
Nourished, watered...
Sky coax out poetic plants -
Cadenced Blossoms:
Graced with thoughts,
Flowered bushes,
Purposeless, save to beautify
The Ten Thousand Things.

~ Kokyo

Restorations

Fresh breezes
Blow through my garden,
This morning -
Looking skyward:
Duch Elm flourishing,
Having survived its disease,
As my dis-ease has flown,
In advance of this restorative Summers' breeze.

~ Kokyo

Wine Cellar

I remember you all,
Those I have loved,
And who've loved me... *
Memories, which I will not lose,
Coloring my heart,
Casting a tapestry of mind;
Carpeting and papering its many chambers;
Leaving me at life's ebb,
Darkly hued-satisfied;
Like mellow burgundy wine-
A cask, a cellar,

To taste, to savor,
Throughout the eternal evening's glow.

~ Kokyo

Weeping Moon

White wafer moon, morning sky,
Mourning our world,
Out of balance, destitute
Perched on the Precipice of Tragedy.

~ Kokyo

Perseverance

Persist, mon ami,
Preserver till overcoming -
Should it seem suffering unrelenting,
Hang to knowledge,
Perseverance in struggle to defeat
The Predator, Scourge of Turmoil;
Yes that persistence to realise
A day without sorrow,
Is an assurance, a guarantor of homecoming.

~ Kokyo

Mozart Piano Concertos

Waterfall, cascading notes,
Dancing, shimmering
In reflected sunlight;
Strings, woodwinds,
Cousining thrills and tremulos;
Capturing summer evening scents,
On wafted breaths of gelide fragrant air...
Woodwinds drift away into darkening shadows.

~ Kokyo

Reflecting Upon Waking From Dream

Remarking, in dream, just now,
On Dylan's
"If Today Was Not an Endless Highway"
I turn, in waking sleep,

To the turn-table at my bedside, in my youth
(The same bed today).

Now, awake, listening to Mendelssohn's,
"Songs Without Words":
4:05 am, this Summer's Morning,
In wonder where my next poem is coming from,
I submit to Ariel once more.

How could I lose those given remembrances?
And, are dreams death's rich Dharmakaya -
Paranirvana's chambers of beauteous wonder?

Down cavernous halls of darker vintage;
The freshness of July nighttime awakening
Engenders, restful, placid, serenity
Reaching eternal joyous surrender.

May all our eternity
Be a refreshing summer's
Dawning into the serenity of the Beautiful -
Darkly Hued.

~ Kokyo

A Blessing

Poems more mellow,

This cloudless night -
No thoughts encroaching -
As a new morning dawns...

Given the sanctity of poetic experience,
Impressing heart/mind,
As fresh morning air caresses our pours,
Like spring riverlets;
How can we refuse to follow her,
Down which-ever path she leads;
Unto river grasses glistening with gladness;
And stunning sunshine startling us into Joy -

May your days be as a morning's berry-picking;
Your evenings spent with your best girl;
And your nights as brief as a summer stroll.

~ Kokyo

Paying Your Dues

Just as we must go through the long,
Tortuous night;
Before we bathe in the warmth,
Of the glistening morning sunshine;
And, just as some poems
Are more beautiful than others;
So we must experience pain and loss,
Simply to enhance the overcoming glades,
Clearing the way,
Giving us grateful days and restful nights.

~Kokyo

Sleep My Princess, Sleep

May you dream as deep and fine,
As the heart that you have to mine entwined.

I watch this early morning,
As you drink the replenishment of slumber,
Hoping you awake to a freshness of heart
Sustaining as the morning's breeze,
Lifts the skirt of the awakening day,

And lands you securely on meadow,
Grassland of heart surety,
Nature's restoration,
Morning mists clearing.

~ Kokyo

Land Ho!

Chirping bird scented morning,

Earlier: plaintive cockeral -
Vouchsave pleasant day's gifted plentitude.

Embarking this day,
Dizzying array of images -
Dazzling panorama of possibilities.

So many grace notes of nuanced impressions;
Having propelled this vessel forward,
Reaching port this settled day;

Guided to lighted harbour,
Waves lapping hull -
This resigned,
And decommissioned summer's eve!

~ Kokyo

Job Description

Universes of poems
Emerge from sacred stirrings in Emptiness;
"Formless fields of benefaction"*
"How vast the robe of liberation"*
Wrapping our hearts in logos,
Freeing living beings...

~ Kokyo
* The Robe Chant (from which, as well, the last two lines are derived)

Something out of Nothing

Smokey-white alderberry flowers,
Sky solid blue, sea of green grass,
Shadowed porch,
Kwan Yin tucked in Cherry Bush:

Sustained upon Dharmakaya,
This consciousness -
Dharmakaya, rather, all in all.
Music entering the formless emptiness,
Which is this panorama:

You see, out of this emptiness,
A form, a poem, has arisen...

~ Kokyo

Shored Against Your Advent

Happy, secure in garden verdure,
Eyes penetrating azure sky;
Purpose, created? Accepted?
Labour leading to Beauty abandoned rest -

Set down upon this Eden,
Offering it to you in poems;
Gather glints and follow,

Nurture nuances of serenity,
To beach upon your birth.

~ Kokyo

Imprinted Footprints

Your trenchant foot prints,
Having passed,
Leading me, pleadingly,
Softly suggesting, with cry
Plaintive, turned to joyous -
Directing me, and mine, home...

~ Kokyo

Morning Haiku

My you always,
Gladden the days

Of those you love
Guiding them to the river of blessed morning.

~ Kokyo David Young

I'll Be There in the Morning

I was with you when we laughed,
And I was there when you cried.
I was with you when your dear one died.
I'll be there with the ebbing of the tide...

But,
I'll be there in the morning,
When the sun shines through the trees;
I'll be there in the evening,
When the trees sing with the cooling breeze.
I'll be there at the closing of the day -
I'll be there when it seems I've gone away...

~ Kokyo David Young

Just Lately

Just lately,
I have lost all, undue, heavy listlessness,
And a light, rest resides within me,

I am relaxed into a hopeful joyousness.
All dread, and anxious anticipation;
All care and pain; all suffering and sorrow,

Departs - an easy heartfelt love & empathy,
Has entered, offering to stay,
Quieting my nights, my days,
Into a relief so sweet, I cannot but feel,
All our crushing times are truly gone,

And the dawn, that knows no evening,
Finally has arrived.

~ Kokyo

Epilogue:

The Cherry Trees in the Garden

You Have My Seal

Give it up,
It will end well,
Your friend needs you,
Give it understanding.

Music eases care,
Bring it to the brink,
Of life, Give your final efforts,
Ending in your loved ones bounty.

You have my seal -
Your days end well,
As all you've loved,
Find their port,
In refuge, the savage sea...

~ Kokyo

I Am Sending You Comfort

I am sending you comfort.
Do something for yourself.
Let the issues ride,

Looking to the inside,
Blooming,
In contrast as the outside's
Looming.

She will fade
Becoming a shade.
Others will go,
You do not know.

~ Kokyo

Residents of the Heart

Tin-can blown down road
Tired till exhaustion
Red dragon's flame extinguished
Fatherland of China transmitted

Memory scanty
Imprinted never flees

In heart residents
Never to depart

~ Kokyo

Glistening in the morning dew,
Their blossoms pinkish white -
The cherry trees along the road!

~ Kokyo

The cherry trees in the garden,
Blown down this winter wind -
Our advancing years!

~ Kokyo

Sitting up after midnight,
Writing poems under the winter moonlight -
The long night expires, with the dawn...

~ Kokyo

The heart is full,
Like the season...
Cherry Blossoms strewn in the wind -

This final poem.

~ Kokyo

November Path

And now the dawn has come,
In-spir-ation has fled,
Tide has torn the pebbles from the shore...

When, the moon re-casts those polished pebbles
Upon a distant shore,
May they, glistening for the feet that tred upon them,
See them safely to that further shore...

~ Kokyo

My Life With Poetry

In my recollection, I had not written a creative word, until, in 1964
George Crawford, my English teacher in grades 11 & 12, discovered I
had a talent for writing. On a piece I had written for an exam he wrote,
.!" He established a prize at graduation for creative writing, and awarded
it to me. When I told him, at that time, I planned to study English
Literature at Dalhousie, he gave me a spontaneous big bear hug.
   From then on my only goal was to become the best writer I could be.
I wrote mostly poetry because, having become ill, that was all I was up
to. Over some years, I build up a body of work and began submitting
them to little magazines, but, with little success. Then I sent a
manuscript of some poems off to London, Great Britain, to
, the Journal of the Buddhist Society. Derek Southall, the editor,
published perhaps, seven; until members of the society objected to his
publishing works not overtly Buddhist.
Resolving to test a theory that I could become published by the little
magazines if I gave them what I thought they wanted, I submitted a
piece, which contained appropriately Canadian images, to

, the little magazine of University of New Brunswick. They took the bait and accepted it.

I continued to evolve my craft; and , by now,

 Crawford, visited my home often, offering help, encouragement, and advice.

I operated on the principle of writing every day no matter how poorly - this was the way to develop style, technique, skill and knowledge. The talent, of course, had to be prerequisite - but one had to put in the work!

Having little luck with further publishing; I gave up in the early 80; perhaps a profound, personal tragedy in my family was a factor in this defeat.

It was not until 2001, with the encouragement of the nurses on the psychiatric ward of the Aberdeen Hospital, that I began once again to write. I published what I wrote then in the newsletter of New Hope Clubhouse. With the arrival of personal computers and tablets, writing and managing my files became so much easier.

I have been writing with fair consistency from then til now, bringing out on Kindle , to date, 4 volumes - 2 of prose & 2 of poetry (3 with this current collection).

My method, as developed, is to wait for a phrase to occur to me; then, increasingly, to write, pausing for my muse to deposit, with some editing, the subsequent phrases and lines, into my empty mind. Sometimes, very often indeed, the phrase occurs to me in sleep; and as I awake and set up my tablet; I run the proposed lines in my mind.

~ Kokyo David Young

The Path Through The Snow
by Kokyo David Young

The awakened way begins as a chill trudge through the snow. We may find the traces of those who have gone before. Even so, our footsteps will, at first, be most tentative. Soon we find ourselves in a forest of confusion; and nightfall brings bitter cold.
With no sense of direction, which way do we turn? Woodland sounds make us anxious; and there is little to forage in the Winter wood.
 Should we become lost like this, our past experience may leave us little means for coping. But, if we are fortunate, we may find shelter and someone to help us find the way.

This is a perfect metaphor for the situation I found myself faced with early in my life; when, entering university, I became severely withdrawn emotionally. And, three years later, after my final year at Dalhousie University, my father was killed one night - run over by his own runaway car, while leaving his office.
These difficulties lead me to Zen.

I was however blessed to find in my frightening forest, a beautiful princess. She became my wife; giving me many gifts, not the least of which was a place to begin Buddhist Practice.
What I gleaned in those early years of practice, issued finally as a sense of the utility of suffering. If we can accept and endure our lot, then we may progress and pass into a clearing in the forest; opening first unto a flowering meadow; then unto a nourishing and beauteous garden.

———————————

Sitting with Suffering

In our lives, whether we are ill or well, we are very often faced with suffering. As a victim of bipolar disorder, the most astounding aspect of my illness was the profound degree of suffering I was experiencing. There was pain of anxiety; astonishing exhaustion; confusion and disruption of conscious experience; isolation and alienation; not to mention the despair of deep depression.

As this began, it quickly became overpowering; crippling; and disabling. It was next to impossible to do anything but lie on the couch racked with anxious pain stinging my brain-stem relentlessly. As my suffering was in my brain there was seemingly no escape.

However, over time, I learned, with the help of proper medication, a technique of bearing my suffering ; of remaining with it, until it dissipated.

Using the method of Zen meditation (known as Zazen), I learned to concentrate my mind so that I was, in time, with daily application, able to hold my emotions in my mind until they naturally dissolved, feeling them fully without reacting to them. By refusing to run from your suffering; by indulging in reckless behaviours, like doing drugs; excessive use of alcohol; or overeating ; or indulging in histrionics - ranting and raving and causing your loved ones so much grief; instead of doing these things, stop, and quietly be with your pain, suffering and anxiety.

The method of Zazen is a gentle, joyous way of sitting, which, once learned, can give lasting benefits of balanced wellbeing.

The Zen master Dogen best depicted the method of Zazen in his Fugen Zazengi :

(Quote)

For practicing Zen, a quiet room is suitable. Eat and drink moderately. Put aside all involvements and suspend all affairs. Do not think "good" or "bad." Do not judge true or false. Give up the operations of mind, intellect, and consciousness; stop measuring with thoughts, ideas, and views. Have no designs on becoming a Buddha. How could that be limited to sitting or lying down?

At your sitting place, spread out a thick mat and put a cushion on it. Sit either in the full-lotus or half-lotus position*. In the full-lotus position, first place your right foot on your left thigh, then your left foot on your right thigh. In the half-lotus, simply place your left foot on your right thigh. Tie your robes loosely and arrange them neatly. Then place your right hand on your left leg and your left hand on your right palm, thumb-tips lightly touching. Straighten your body and sit upright, leaning neither left nor right, neither forward nor backward. Align your ears with your shoulders and your nose with your navel. Rest the tip of your tongue against the front of the roof of your mouth, with teeth together and lips shut. Always keep your eyes open, and breathe softly through your nose.

Once you have adjusted your posture, take a breath and exhale fully, rock your body right and left, and settle into steady, immovable sitting. Think of not thinking. Not thinking-what kind of thinking is that? Non-thinking. This is the essential art of zazen. ....

When you arise from sitting, move slowly and quietly, calmly and deliberately. Do not rise suddenly or abruptly. In surveying the past, we find that transcendence of both mundane and sacred........sitting or standing have all depended entirely on the power of zazen.....

,...... ....intelligence or lack of it is not an issue; make no distinction between the dull and the sharp-witted. If you concentrate your effort single-mindedly, that in itself is wholeheartedly engaging the way.

Practice-realization is naturally undefiled. Going forward is, after all, an everyday affair.
(Close Quote)

~ Kokyo David Edgar Young

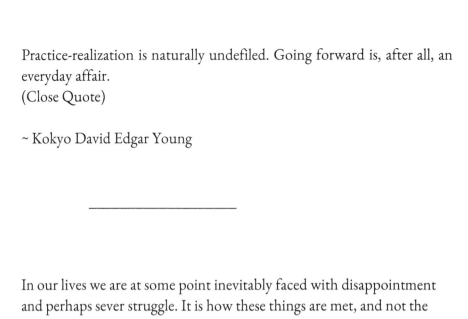

In our lives we are at some point inevitably faced with disappointment and perhaps sever struggle. It is how these things are met, and not the fact of their occurrence, which determines outcome.
We can face obstacles with acceptance and determination to find the solution that lies hidden, but implicit, in the problem.
This act of discovery and implementation of solutions, is what creates the pearl. The irritant, the grain of sand in the oyster, is the necessary precursor to Joy.
Turn stumbling blocks into stepping stones.

~ Kokyo David Edgar Young

Becoming Clear

Faint sunlight through faded drapes,
Parting curtains -

Bright Day!

~ Kokyo

Does the layer of ice
Know its own beauty
In reflecting sunlight?

~ Tesshin

Unknown to itself,
the beauty of the sunlight,
reflected in my heart.

~ Kokyo

Poem of Appreciation
(for Dr Randy Burrill)

Physician, you brought me from ill to well;
You restored me to my life;
Preventing my mind's ultimate collapse.

You directed my wife & I to peaceful pasture;
Granting us the means to flourish;
Establishing us in mutual patience.

A Bodhisattva, you, of medicine,
Compassion beyond measure;
A Doctor in the finest tradition -
Not unlike my progenitor.

Physician; Bodhisattva; Friend.

~ Kokyo David Young

Poet as Aeolian Harp

In Samadhi, I offer myself,
As an aeolian harp.

Sunshine registers;
As also, wind & grief.

I bend out to the fair breeze
And the violent torrent.

Use me,
Till the sounding board's exhausted.

~ Kokyo

embers in the fire die -
a glow, a warmth, a radiance,
and then is gone...
stir, with a stick, in these ashes...

In sleep, I slip away,
The trail, twists, curls,
Is gone...

~ Kokyo

Pictou , Nova Scotia.........July 26/2018

A Tincture of
Morning Sunshine

Poems by
Kokyo David Young

~ For my son Shawn ~

Morning Sun

So fine,
to sit
in the morning sunshine -

Dog passes by,
wagging his tail

Not so inclined,
I go inside,
with the obscuring cloud.

~ Kokyo

Kernel of Ease

Sakyamuni's arena of suffering - Samsara,
Encompassed by ether of Nirvana.
Within - birth, old age, sickness,and death
The field of bodhisattva practice - skillful means,
Functions permeated by bodhi, Buddha Nature.

In storm, we find kernel of Ease…
From strain, extract Release…

Stroll through dewy, morning meadow,
Into memory, glistening with eternity.

~ Kokyo

A Walk, a Picnic

When I walk with Emily,
She always balances on the curb
As I hold her hand.
Coming to a Sandy Shoal, we beachcomb,
Gathering flotsam and jetsam
In a bucket we come across.

On to the library to search "Dora the Explorer",
Then, up the hill to the Academy's gazebo -
We picnic as she translates the crows caws.

Summer in winter of old age,
Sunshine in dark of night.
Eternity shimmering with memories.

~ Kokyo

Gape

Gape for new love -
Shine your morning sun;
Mix the intimate brew…

Fan the fading cinders -
Foster bonfires of flux;
Gather returns of closing days.

~ Kokyo

A Poem for My Wife

We, you and I dear,
Are close -
Like two fingers crossed,
We cover each other's bond.

If one of us dies,
The other soon follows -
We cannot live apart.

We have been so long by each other's side;
We breathe like the tide -
The sighing of the waves is like our breathing -
Sea to shore.

That pain in our hearts
Is the grating of pebbles
Being torn from the shore…

Our last breaths, at ebb-tide…

~ Kokyo

Sunyata

Sometime, there will be

, for you,
Tomorrow will not come -
The day will no longer progress,
And their will be no more night.
Your body will drop off,
There will be no where, no when -
Eternally, when there is no longer a breath,
A hush, an abatement, an

,
Will forever, contain,
Will
 our Joy.

~ Kokyo

Listening for her traces
In the cold winter night -

Peacefully, pages are turned…

~ Kokyo

Peacefully Noticing The Apocalypse

Sitting in the early morning's
Apocalyptic haze
(Like Nero we fiddle with our phones
While the world ignites)
The cry of "Jobs! Jobs!"
Becoming our death knell.

~ Kokyo

(email to my Sensei)

Learning the teachings of age & conditions,
Dropping off dross,
Accepting and going beyond .

Returning to the beach of my beginnings;
Strolling in this aged garden -
Simplified in studied grace…

~ Kokyo

Soon - Spring (an emblem)

Soon spring comes,
Color returns to earth,
Stretch forth our being.

Huddled in cold,
We remember, vaguely, ardor and gladness -
Hidden now, we grope in winter's shadows.

The melt, the thaw, arrives,
Proclaim yellow sun,
Gentle warmth, stunning sky.

~ Kokyo

no longer seek the stunning line,
study rather subdued simplicity.

~ Kokyo

A Phrase of Mozart

Piano Concerto No. 6 in B-Flat Major, K 238,
Head spins ajar - suddenly,
New fabric of consciousness:

Transnatation, inchoate element…
Amorphous, nebulous,
Yet new cleft brought into being -

Contented

~ Kokyo

Roaming in the world of words,
In mind's garden harvesting
The
;
My kindle is my seed catalogue.

~ Kokyo

Kwan Yin Sits

Kwan Yin sits in our emotional squalor,
Mitigating our turmoil.
Gathering your aspirations,
Casting them at her feet…

She beaches your concern on the further shore
Sanding smooth your tired brain,
Revealing your minds finer grain.
Allow the cleansing compassion -
Project release upon the void.

~ Kokyo

I have carried my burden long and far,
Someday soon I will lay it, with a thud! -
On the sand of the further shore…

~ Kokyo

Valiant Heart

I have given you a valiant heart -
Long you foraged in the dark.
Then I brought you to the sun,
Which you shone on everyone…

~ Kokyo

Styx

Time of Turmoil
Awakening one morning,
Pronouncing myself Mad,
Pain gnawed at my helpless brain.
Cast into a foreign manner of experience,
A haunting mode of torture and torment
Began, to last 20 years unceasingly.

Withdrawn into lack of self,
Unable to speak save for practical matters -
"pass the salt".
Exhaustion, fracturing of thought,
Alienation, frozen will.
Disabling illness, death,

Outcast from human association.

Saved by Ruby, my wife, my Kwan Yin,
Rebuilding, rediscovery,
Reinstatement of mind…

Bridge over the river Styx

~ Kokyo

Voyageur

Launched at sunrise,
Leopold was easily lifted.
However legends differ,
If the weather was inclement.

Years into his journey,
Finding his esthetic sense,
He found a companion, Gerty,
To ease his lonely hours.
Comely, she soothed him;
He aspired. He walked
Each evening to her door…

But conditions congealed harshly -
They parted.
         ………

Mind collided with menacing peril.
Music conjoined to dissonant confusion.
As anxious rodents scuffed across
His heart's furfuraceous floor.

         ………

He came at last to the terminus of his travels
To the land of emeralds,
Where Kwan Yin, Molly, scooped him up
In her tender compassionate hands.

Now, retiring in the evening sun,
They, having released their doves,
Beach their tiny craft, assuredly,
Upon the pliant other shore.

They have travelled...

~ Kokyo

Caught on the cusp,
Then, cuffed to the curb!

~ Kokyo

Watching my mind crumble;
Feeling the pain run 'round my heart -
I am thankful that I am mortal.

~Kokyo

Zazen (2)

In Buddha Chamber:
Refreshing breezes,

Cooling wave -

No concerns

~ Kokyo

Old Dead Days

Past times - some live; others decay.
All our days spent,
Shed like forlorn tears.

Old dead days,
Roll into crypt;
While today unfolds in cool expanse.

Remnants of fire -
Gathered glimpses of splendor.

~ Kokyo

A Slouched off Skin

Death is not just the history
Of our brokenness -
Ruts along our passing
Of the way;

But,
The trail of our triumphs -
It is but… *

~ Kokyo
* indicates that death is an interruption of life

Nascency

Corrupt scent of Autumn leaves -
Natural death, ongoing recurrence.
(Accident not easily accepted).

Bodily functions fail defilement due.
Putrefaction replenishes compost earth.

Earth nurtures living;
life prompts parturition.*

~ Kokyo
* been using my thesaurus ☐

Meaning muted;
Poet approaches pointlessness…

Choice

I like having a choice
Among coffee, green tea, and Earl Grey;
I like that I have a choice
Between Toscanini biography;
Re-reading a Margaret Lawrence novel,
And many other books.

Resting when I like;
Reading when able;
Music at will, anything at all ever recorded!

Choosing dinner; zazen, etc -
Although limited in old age,
I like that I still have plenty of choice.

~ Kokyo

When the Music Stops

Will you be watching TCM;
Or texting Madison;
Will you be shingling a roof;
Reading George Martin;
Lecturing on Rousseau;
At an orchestral concert;
Or cleaning up a bed?

When the Music stops,
How will you ever find the playlist;
Who will you appeal to for the title;
Or where will you seek that clever line?

In silence of snowy afternoon;
Or aching, empty, windy, summer night;
Breathless autumnal shower;
And rebirth of springtime daffodils ;
Will there begin an echo of bounty,
And will you hear again,
Music sounding softly in your soul?

~ Kokyo

Dissonance

Distracted from watching, calmly (on tablet),
Mozart's Dissonance String Quartet video;
By jarring rant of bigot on Law & Order -

I wonder where the 'dissonance '
Truly lies?

~ Kokyo

Trout Fishing in Canada

"Walk this way, please."
I followed down the bank of the stream.

"Drop your line here, in this deep, dark pool,
By the edge - they sleep here in the cool."
I always obeyed.

He taught by his gentleness;
I learned to take his pace -
To view from the bluff, as he.
Like he, I was cut down early.
I made my bed on the threshold.

She said, "We should get together."
I followed her many leagues -
I learned, we grew.
We made our camp on the heartland.
Our fires always burning…

"Come, here inside this hut."
Here, we spread our breakfast table -
Here we cooked our meals, many were fed.
We made our watch into the night,
Hearth upon the headland.

"Many are cold; but few are frozen!"

~Kokyo

Opening Unto the Expanse

We drove up the street tonight
Where, fifty years ago
You were killed.

Castle Clear shattered into shreads,
Now, collected, shiny trinkets
Gathered in the closets.

"If, wonderling,
You are ready, we might proceed,
Huddling in the night;
Seeking further insight."

When we were twenty, we were fragmentary.
We follow along into the night…   …   …
Dawn, now, beckons
While my reckoning continues -

"When will the knock
Occur at the door?"

"What comes forth
When there is no where, no when?
When time is no longer; and no shorter?"

Meanwhile it is best
To keep active passively.
To endeavor without effort.
Being living; emitting everything ,
Denying; affirming…
Toes twitching, fingering our chins.

If ever you see me crossing the bay,
In the summer moonlight;
Or striding down the backroad -
Mind cast upon the night sky
Universe hung with lights;
Leaves shimmering, quivering -
Then capture it with your smartphone,
And, please, tag it your friends.
And to me!

~ Kokyo

Poem for My Wife

We, you and I dear,
Are close -
Like two fingers crossed,
We cover each other's bond.

If one of us dies,
The other soon follows -
We cannot live apart.

We have been so long by each other's side;
We breathe like the tide -
The sighing of waves is like our breathing -
Sea to shore.

That pain in our hearts,
Like grating of pebbles
Being torn from the shore…

Our last breaths, at ebb-tide…

~ Kokyo

Rake the fallen leaves of hope -
Our fires may inspire,
Lest we expire.

~ Kokyo

Compassionate Heart

It is the heart of compassion to care;
But, through over extension,
Our hearts may break -

There comes a point where to share more pain,
Becomes unbearable.
Where do our hearts go from here?

This is what I hope to explore.

~ Kokyo

Baking Biscuts

Bakin' biscuts,
Despite no strength,
Say' "I ain't done!"

~ Kokyo

How Long

Auschwitz was the true extreme.
I am not justified to cry of a broken heart;
And yes, as yet, I feel it healing -
Ruby keeps it warm
Emily keeps it warm
Shawn & Karen keep it warm.
 is the source of that love.
Where or how came the log jam?
What the blockage?
Why the watercourse interrupted on its way?
Sectarian dogmatism; bigotry, ignorance and hate.
The writing
Gracing the wall is seen as desecration.
The greedy, selfish, narcissist
Persist unchecked…
What reason to hope?

We must guard and heal our hearts,
Proceeding from our doorsteps kindly,
Mending our dashed hope,
We muster, we rally,
Not a battle cry,
But when the fascists call,
We answer, pleading, without rancor,
"How Long?"
With each call,
We will answer, without rancor,

""How long?"

~ Kokyo

Die Unsullied

I am old and I am tired,
I have seen a nation's children,
Taken from their parents,
And locked in cages -
Think of it...Think of it…

The fascists rise,
Decency leaves the public square…
Heed not the message of polarization;
Let our commonality predominate.

Seas of calamity rise,
Tsunami of oppression threaten;
Discourse dies; placards beat asunder.

Models of kindness;
Gentlemen & Gentlewomen,
By persistent example must prevail.
(Adopt the coheresive manner,
And you have been co-oped…)

Die with dignity,
And the fascists conquer nothing -
They wish to turn you into them. Then die.

~ Kokyo

Threatening Clouds*

It is duty, to be placid;
Error, to be enraged.

I hope to sit in my garden
In spring & summer,
Calm, despite what goes on,
Beyond my property..

Sit in your garden,
However you fashion your retreat,
Your sanctuary,
Even if found only in your heart/mind -

Be kind, unwinding your concerns;
We must rest tonight for tomorrow threatens.
I wait before the garden gate,
Someday we spread our blanket -
A picnic, a gentle dinning in the evening,
When "the threatening clouds have passed away".

~ Kokyo
*

Colored Leaves as Compost

Rake these colored leaves as compost,
Into your hearts' garden.
After necrosis they nurture future fullness.

Not growing grotesque,
Apply nutrients your hearts' soil -
Rid your bed of noxious weeds…

Foster color and variety,
Lush with luster, let our gardens be…

~ Kokyo

Rudimentary Thoughts

...no, it is precisely this "limp-wristed"
response which is needed.
The "strong arm" has got us into this mess!

By acquiescence, by sitting when others stand;

....but I am apolitical, I am a poet,
I can throw the boot off my neck only by stealth,
Unspoken patience, and diligence -
My sphere is management of the subjugated spirit:
You see, they cannot have our minds.
They cannot have our minds!

~ Kokyo

Nature's Persistent Beauty

She continues to beautify herself,
Despite our abuse.
Like her, we offer up beauty to obscure the ugly;
Congenitality to nullify depravity;
Serenity to confound the raging torrent.

~ Kokyo

Spend this Hour with Me

Spend an hour with Me,
In your garden;
And I will give you a poem,
Beyond compare:

Old friends hearten;
Nature gladdens;
Greening leaves give eternal hope -
Although sun be temporarily obscured,
Darkening cloud soon disperses,
Allowing expanse of azure blue.

A moment in the sun -
Then silence hushes all sorrow
Joy prevailing ever…

~Kokyo

A Heart which Rises Up

Give us a heart which rises up;
Our spirit, a boat with nets which comprehend.

We are such, with evolving heart/minds,
Growing, becoming…
But encapsulated in words -
Why, it promotes misunderstanding,
The word fostering hate and death -
Death of heart; death of spirit;
Death of understanding.

This is why the book was sealed.
This is why this poem has ended

~ Kokyo

Garden Itself Paling

Morning shelter;
Splendid sunlit warmth -
Already the fading forsythia!

~ Kokyo

Master's Voice

The reticence of encroaching death,
Masters rising…
Speech perverting meaning -
To proclaim is to preclude.

Our experience mulled;
Smelting away our dross -
An empty fullness ascending…

~ Kokyo

Poem for Tesshin

Morning zazen in rain -
Fresh rivulets enter my garden,
Once again!

Gassho,

~ Kokyo

Hojo-san,

It is the nature of compassion
To grieve -
To be broken....

Oh, look,
The shattered mirror on the bodhi stand -
Each piece a resurrected Buddha!

Gassho,

~ Kokyo

Rainy morning,
Grey sky -
I apply myself to study.

~ Kokyo

S

For: Bernie White, Steve Harder, Earl Love, & Marylin McCormick,
with thanks

And in loving memory of Shannon & James Fraser

Spring vs Winter

In spring, to love,
Is easy;
Easy also, to be kind.

Winter, when beauty has fled;
Needs learned patience & forbearance,
One must make a silent gift of reticence.

Winter, the best study of the way;
For true happiness is the issue
Of compassionate tenderness;
And kindness is more succulent when aged.

~ Kokyo

God's Intelligence

God is clever and shrewd in his ways -
Trust in him is proven true;
He anticipates the outcome of our trust.

He is with me in the morning, at noon,
And at night -
He will not fail me, even if I perish
I will reside with him and my loved ones.

All of you who crave him will be filled;
Those who call him, in sincerity & conviction
Shall recieve his blessing,
Waiting and trusting in Him.

~ Kokyo

Maturity

Dao has ordered
Things wondrously, for me -
In the fullness of time:
He discovers me to myself.

~ Kokyo

Love

Love, beyond human understanding
Known to the heart -
"Will you be coming home with me tonight?"
Softly, "Yes"

Many mansions perfectly ordered -
Jealousy overruled by fealty.

~ Kokyo

Battle over,
Victory won,
Hero, traveled courageously -
Peacefully in garden

Kokyo

An ignorant man
Convinced of his own intelligence -
Slow to evolve

~ kokyo

Allow rumble of motorcycle/truck
Injure you.
Do not resist -
Vexation lies in resistance.

~ Kokyo

Heaven's Moon

I was given heaven's moon tonight,
After quiet dialogue with infinite spirit.

Orange chinese lantern,
Hung in horizon -

The cosmos, wondrously
phenomenal, with ultra-mundane beauty.

~ Kokyo (circa 5:00 am July 16/2019)

(For my dear Friend, Lum Weng Kong)

Master Lum,
Keeper of the Buddha Heart -

On rice paper,
Rendered!

~ Kokyo

I Have Watched...

I watched a man die as I held his gaze.
My own father was killed by his runaway car.
My great grandfather
Was trampled by runaway team of horses,
While he saved children in their path.
And I have know other unspeakable tragedy.
While gnats ate my brain away from the inside -
,
I have kept my Joy.

I sit in the sun,
And I ponder the imponderables,
And my heart aches.
As my body ceases;
My mind searches for comfort,

But how can I be comforted when children suffer?
,
Can I keep my Joy?

I will bend out into the world,
Compassionate till suffering ends,
 this very Compassion will be my Joy.

~ Kokyo

Phoenix

While you were talking, just now,
I suddenly saw again the fresh, young girl,
Sweet in her joyousness,
The girl I originally fell in love with, years ago.

It brought to mind the Zen phrase:
"What you are speaks so loud,
I can't hear what you say," -
For I have no knowledge of what you said.

But I know that,
While you were talking this evening,
So animatedly,
I fell in love with you all over again."

~ all my love, always,

The Poet wrote the following line:

Moon shines down into waiting harbour…

But, Poet, could go no further,
Having lost his voice…

Seems he became too entranced with the moon,

Longing to be where moon was…

Poet inquired of his neighbour, Zhuang Zi,
Who loaned him the bird Peng,
Who carried him up into the limitless expanse.

Up in the boundless he became intoxicated,
On the thin air and could no longer see the earth..

(He was fine so long as he could enjoy the emptiness;
But when he tried to venture
Out of the Poison Cave in which he was trapped,
He couldn't function,
He was clumsy and confused.)

Exploring his cave,
He came upon a fierce fire-breathing dragon, Qi.
The energy of Qi's fire consumed him,
Burning away the dross,
Base metals of his nature.

In time he learned of Qi's benevolence;
Tamed him, and rode on his back
Returning to earth..

On earth, finding his proper place,
Viewing the heavens from earth,
He saw the insubstantial colors
Of the Ten Thousand Things -
He found his voice,
And was able to complete his poem:

Moon shines in bright night on shimmering waters-
Poet sits on pier viewing summer scene -
Lost in beauty glistening harbour.

~ Kokyo

On Meeting Old Friends

Since last we met,
We have grown old, my friends -
Our gait is rusty, and our minds fade.

A long road we have walked together.
But now, I see, on this final way -
A more personal journey,
We must take, alone…

But, when we meet again,
Upon reaching our several destinations,
We will exalt in each other's company,
As of old...

~ Kokyo

Late Day Reflection

Sun shining specially on her son,
This afternoon -
Family collected on the

Hovering 'tween
 &
 -
Repletion!

~ Kokyo

A Mother's Death

At your death, things were so

.
We had spent two years together,
Grieving Dad;
We had become close, compassionate
To each other.

Yet, at your death, things were so unsettled.
What would be his uncertain future?
And I felt your bitter feelings…

Of course, now, my life having been retrieved;
You,
, watching as you do,
So much has since been settled -
The relationship has certainly continued -
And we are firm in our minds,
Our hearts resonate out to each other
And to

.

And it is placid to anticipate a further communion,
Unhampered, unsullied, serene -
Dedicated to those who remain ungathered...

~ David

(Devolution is its Own Solution)

Youth is the right time -
But it has no time for illness.
You and I were fine;
But our health came between us.

 (The last time I saw you,
You fell away like an avalanche.
But, by then I knew all was ended,
And I lost my grip to hold you -
The landscape terrified me,
I was spending an unknowing currency)

All else being equal -
There would have been a sequel.
As it was, there was no way,
And we were meant for disappointment.

~ Kokyo (son of Fraser)

My Histrionics

My histrionics,
Occasioned by my illness,
Caused you great grief,
My wife, my parents, my son…

You bore me great forbearance,
But they cut like words into stone,
By a ruthless chisel.

You kept faith,
You invested in our futures.
You forgave.

If I have atoned,

It was by patience and circumspection,
Giving you, by kind action,
I trust, a reason to rejoice.

~ Kokyo

The Free Way

I have long been free.
I was not always so.

We are determined by our lot;
By sexual allure;
By our genetic makeup and our conditions.
However,
Within the functioning framework of these -
We can be free.

By acceptance, by practice,
By walking the way we become free
Of the way.

~Kokyo

Hemorrhagic Compassion

A crises of compassionate pain and suffering;
The only sustainable position
In this hemorrhaging world.

Suffering, in and beyond volition;
As balm for this plague of evil contagion -
A remedy for the otherwise powerless:

Care beyond caring until caring overcomes.

~ Kokyo

Death Creeps

Death creeps insidious
Throughout this carcass;
As this haggard brain falters,
Mind awaiting body's demise -

Like a placenta,
This animal will be discarded,
While Heart finds release…

~Kokyo

The Spit Of…

Skip into the dark of night
Slipping into the dawning light…

Waltz 'round; high step; cake walk,
Back to fields' wild flowers plenty.
Meeting you, need not talk.

Many fallow gardens empty
Rest in unity extinction's serenity -
Extending. ..

~ Kokyo

Chasing Chimera

As I see it,
The problem is

Dementia, no,
Depression, no,
My wife, no,

My weight, no
My sedentary nature, no,

Camus absurd, no,
Trump, hell no,

Life sucks, no,
Then it's arthritis,

Hell it's all of the above -
Everybody's got it hard -
Get over yourself -
Listen to your Brahms!!

~ Kokyo

When I Get Home

I won't have to listen to any more bullshit;
Nor countenance evil -
When I get home.

Not having a body there will be no more pain;
And I may reach out compassionately,
To the World -
When I am home.

My family will suffer the loss;
And there is no rationalizing their grief;
But they will resolve more easily their issues -
When I get home.

I may wait in serenity for your arrival;
And see the engine of the world's travail,
And work to its resolution -
When I get home.

This is the
Kokyo

I am tired now
And I can't help you as I used to -
What is worse,
Compassion comes hard now.

I don't like this,
It is part of desolation;
And my body impedes my heart/mind.

And out of habit, and desire
I try to spin this to a upbeat conclusion:
After death there is no impediment.

~ Kokyo

For my dear friends Quam & Laurene
And for, Lum Weng Kong-san - Master Artist!

Pink sound of summer breezes
Sailng across Weigela...
Refreshing,
Like your recent visit!

~ Kokyo
(for Tesshin)

Sweet bird twittering high in tree -
Summons summer sunshine!

~ Kokyo

Damp of early morning:
Bird, to his lover,
Plaintively sings -

Devotion.

~ Kokyo

In damp of early dawn,
Bird calls, unceasingly -

Hopeless

~ Kokyo

Mountain stream meanders its way -
Impediments accommodating.

~ Kokyo

Family of three,
Pass in succession:
Ragged, from difficult days -

Blessings!

~ Kokyo

Little bird,
thank you for your song, nourishing,
on this beauty-haunted evening…

~ Kokyo

Little green worm,
I've wondered where you've been -
I am glad you have not gone extinct.

~ Kokyo

Divination

At dawn,
Awake, writing poetry -

Birds tweet
I have the
!

~ Kokyo (5:15 am july 16/2019)

Early Morning,
In my garden,
Waiting for poem to occur -

Coromants fly to fish at Caribou Island!

~ Kokyo

Pigeons on line above dappled willow:
Red insulating feet -

Gone, with fleeting morning!

~ Kokyo

I go in just now to lay down;
Not hearing neighborhood children screeching -

Perverse dissatisfaction
at not finding annoyances.

~ Kokyo

Refreshment of summer rain-
Life-restoring fragrance!

~ Kokyo

Brown wooden Buddha,
Flowerless Altar -
Too old to tend my garden.

~ Kokyo

Swirl of bird song -
Do they sing to Chopin?

~ Kokyo

One Big Mistake

In dream,
Ruby & I examine old photos -

All my life,
I've paid attention to the wrong things.

~ Kokyo

Calligraphy

Ready -
Ink -
Stain the paper -
Savor

Darkness -
Think -
Flood of light -
Night

~ Kokyo

□ □□□

Denouement:

Like a stray cat,
I leave these
 at your doorstep -

To prove I am hunting for you!

~ Kokyo

Foraging for poetry our hearts are ravished -
Our missteps glare in the night…

~ Kokyo

A warm summer's rain
Has hung a mist on the glen;
Upon opening the drapes I am cheered.

~ Kokyo

Light of company
In dark of winter -
Lonely now party is over...

~ Kokyo

Fragment

A jaundiced eye peppers my replies
Forth into winter winds and frosts…

In cold mornings, icy feet tread grass.
Clutched by grace, climb unto the setting sun -
Oasis of light in darkening world;

~ Kokyo

For my wife Ruby

Ghosts

We dealt with the ghosts of the two world wars;
We dwelt with the harm of that surfacing of evil.
We fought our father's battles in our night terrors.

Our faltering gate leading to madness.

With minds askew, our hearts hankered love.
We swept along the dark night beach with the wind,
Watching the town on the harbour's edge;
Expiating ghosts into blessedness.

Generations before and since berailed us as shiftless.
Our artists and poets grappled with the perplexities
Of an experience howling in a nightmarish world;
Coursing into a booming abyss of oblivion.

We dealt with the ghosts of the great world wars;
We dwelt with the harm of that surfacing of evil.
We fought our father's battles in our night terrors.
Our faltering gate leading to madness.

We have emptied dust into the void;
We have ground our nascent elixir into pollen;
We brush against the eternal with our soiled hearts,
Hanging our Joy in the umbrella-stand, till morning.

~ Kokyo David Young

Hanging by a Thread to the Absolute

Exhausted.
Hanging by a thread to the absolute -
Relying on the
 to maintain.
Dependant upon the source,
To stay the course.

No need to idly dither.

~ Kokyo

Is it the night of the full August moon?
It is 1972,
The poet is devastated by illness profound -
A fertile ferment is occurring…

Bright blighted night,
Northern nights invite those gathered
Be still and know their God!

Artists assembled, Brothers Poets and Witches.
Announcement unheard, promise unheeded.

The full moon of January '73
Sky broken open - poet released.
The gifted bodhisattva soon arrives...
Enchantment brought to earth.

Now the trouble really begins -
Death Madness Mayhem and Murder.
Illness Dissension and Death

Their latter full moons will deliver
Decline of senses & mobility.
Gently they stroke each other in the night.
Lulled into submission and blessedness.

Encouraging and comforting
Entering the final gate…
Suffering as ever, but, as ever -
Courage and consolation in the light.

Steadfast she moves for him;
Aware he remains for her….
Being as one.

~ Kokyo

Rather have a heart than be heartless,
To be torn by compassion,
Shorn of composure,
Preferable to being impervious to caring.

Better to be susceptible to pain;
And buffeted by news of atrocities,
Than buffered and sheltered,
And miserable and miserly in heart.

~ Kokyo

Parsifal

Struck by a stray metaphor -
A slashing wound, bitting
Shrapnel images opened his vivid side.

Clamoring to the sea bank,
He called for a medic;
Passing out -
To an ocean of fish
Named after schooling poets…

William Carlos Williams swam by
Looking for his mistress meter;
Ryokan circled begging for daily occurrences
With a bowl he found last morning;
While shark Shakespeare circled,
Devouring
As the medic dressed his wound with garlic
And bound him with reworked doggerel

Awakening in hospital,

His nurse, Jade,
Administering to his open gash
With a lance of pure poetic mercy,
Inspired him to write musical verse
Which he titled Good Friday Music.

He became a pacifist.

~ Kokyo

Our sole companions,the birds,
This cool northern morning…
Our voices draped in icey dew.

~ Kokyo

end

Printed in Great Britain
by Amazon